1999

For Leona,

Best Wishes,

Tom Cecil

I WANT
MY TURN
IN THE
SHOWER

——— ———

Tom Cecil

Printed in the United States of America

Second printing
10 9 8 7 6 5 4 3
January 1999

Library of Congress Catalog Card Number 96-97136

ISBN 0-925436-14-3

Cam-Tech
P.O. Box 341
Fletcher, OH 45326

This book is dedicated to my family:
Mary, Mike, Amy, Matt, Martha, Rebecca, Nancy and Phebe
and
To my father, Lester L. Cecil,
who taught me to write,
and my mother, Celia Cecil,
who taught me to laugh.

CONTENTS

Introduction

With this book Tom Cecil has chosen to be remembered by his family and friends as a writer of wit and perhaps humor.

I find it difficult to decide whether Tom's collection of columns is one or the other.

To appreciate wit requires an educated mind in the reader as well as the writer, because wit makes use of literary references, puns and paradoxes. One does not laugh at wit. One admires it with the lift of an eyebrow or a half smile of appreciation.

Humor is more middle class than wit, and in Tom's stories of being a father to seven children, you will find more humor than wit.

This is not a book to be read straight through. Take it with you to read while you wait in line at the tax department or any other branch of the government. It's good for whiling away the waiting time at the doctor's office or the dentist's. Read one chapter at night when you can't sleep. Work your way through it slowly. It requires savoring.

Some of these pieces will give you quiet pleasure. Some of them may catch you off guard and cause chuckles or hiccups.

On second thought, I believe the book is a felicitous combination of wit and humor.

Roz Young

Acknowledgments

First, I want to thank my family for unknowingly contributing to many of these columns just by being there. They served as grist for my mill.

My thanks are also due to the newspapers that published my guest columns: Amos Publications, especially the *Kettering-Oakwood Times*, *Centerville-Bellbrook Times* and *The Beavercreek News Current*; The Journal Herald and the Dayton Daily News; and Bolling-Moorman Publications with newspapers in Tipp City, West Milton, New Carlisle, Huber Heights, Englewood, Trotwood, Troy, Vandalia and Brookville.

Next, the tremendous effort of Terri Carr should be noted. Terri was my legal secretary for many years. Her gentle nudging kept files moving from my desk to hers and then back to me. Terri is now a desktop publisher. In preparing the manuscript for this book, she spent countless hours at her computer as I wrote and rewrote.

I also want to thank Bill Bombeck for permitting me to use quotes of Erma Bombeck throughout this book and for furnishing the photo of Erma.

Randy Palmer is a professional artist and illustrator who is on the staff of the *Dayton Daily News*. His illustrations have given my text another dimension and kept this book focused on the lighter side of life.

Tom Cecil

Preface

For many years I secretly desired to write a book. But I never thought it would happen in this lifetime, which come to think of it, is the very best lifetime in which to write. Occasionally, someone suggested that I write a book. At these times I always reneged, trying to do it with a proper dose of humility.

Then several months ago I read an anecdote that made me think. A sculptor was asked how he created such a beautiful polar bear. "It was easy," he explained. "I just removed everything that didn't look like a polar bear." Although creating a polar bear would be impossible in my case, I pondered whether I might write a book by removing from a stack of my guest columns all of those that didn't look like a book.

Anything is worth a shot, I reasoned, so I sorted my writings into two stacks. One stack was called "looks like a book" and the other I dubbed "doesn't look like a book." As you confront the rest of this book, you might wonder if I mixed the stacks.

I have tried to address three main themes in this book. First is the humor we find in everyday situations. Second is the frustration that taxpayers experience at the hands of a nonresponsive government. Although I was born into a Republican and conservative family in 1927, I have a great respect for our two-party system of government. Third, I have written testimonials to two people for whom I have great respect—Erma Bombeck, a dear friend, and my father, Lester L. Cecil.

Where does one find humor? My oldest son, Mike, had a cubbyhole in the back seat of our station wagon facing the rear. While I was driving home from church one Sunday, he announced, "Hey, Dad, you better speed up. There's a cop right behind you." Kids say the funniest things without even trying. I decided to listen to mine, not only to avoid traffic tickets, but also to harvest one of the best sources of humor a parent can find: his own children. I'm convinced that families need to laugh more.

My youngest daughter, Phebe, was three years old when she

first experienced corn on the cob. With butter running down her cheeks, hands and arms, she thrust the empty cob toward me and said, "Put more on it, Daddy." In her childish innocence, she thought daddies could do anything.

In addition to one's own family, another source of humor is people, wherever they are and whatever they're doing. And every day the news media prints or broadcasts material cast in a lighter vein. Further sources are politicians, whose humor is often astronomically expensive for taxpayers.

Early art, still visible today on walls of caves, tells us that our ancestors wanted to transcend time. They're saying they spent time on this earth and they have a message. I've never been quite sure what that message was, but I know they wanted to communicate with us. In the same way, I hope this book might transcend my life and speak to people in the next century and millennium.

But I'm a realist and therefore understand that this book, either in a store or in your home, will have a short shelf life. Some copies will be used to prop up one of the legs on your card table; others on the kitchen counter will serve as a hot pad; some might become projected missiles as daughter number two slings it at son number one; some of the books will end up on the night stand of your guest room where they will seldom be touched by human hands. Not to be forgotten is the garage sale where, for a dollar bill or fifty cents, the owner will gladly part with his copy.

This is not meant to be "a book you can't put down." You can easily put it aside, but I hope you'll pick it up again. Mainly, I don't want you to yawn off before page 10. Maybe you'll chuckle now and then, choke up at sad parts and be challenged to rise up against some of the absurdities that dot our political landscape.

I

CHILDREN—
THEY SHARPEN THEIR TEETH ON YOU

Drought
My daughter's home from school;
I can tell it by the shower.
I only get my turn
After she's been there an hour.

Two opposing concepts confront us as parents with respect to our children. One theory claims they are a gift from God. Conversely, W.C. Fields said, "Anyone who hates children and dogs can't be all that bad." Between these two ideas is a vast gray area. Most parent-child relationships fall within these parameters.

Yes, there are days when you truly believe your children are a gift from God. A daughter runs in breathlessly from the first grade. "Mommy, I can read," she exclaims. Your son greets you in the driveway after work. "Daddy," he explodes, "I can ride my two-wheeler without help." On Mother's Day the kindergartner pops into the house with something—maybe a pin box—with handmade pictures. On Father's Day the kids deliver your breakfast in bed along with the Sunday paper. Never mind that you can't identify what's on your plate. On a Saturday night you scrub the kids up and the next day they look almost angelic sitting between you in church. Of course, on a few occasions a youngster puts the offering plate in his lap, throws in a crumpled dollar bill and pulls out coins until he feels good about his gift. Of course, all eyes in the surrounding pews are riveted on your son, who thinks he's got all day to make the transaction.

But there are those not-so-good days when the company has arrived early for dinner and is visiting in the living room. A kid yells from upstairs, "Hey, Mom, all I can find are clean towels up here. OK if I use one?" A pre-toddler, sometimes referred to as a

1

"rug rat" or "anklebiter," pulls a cord, causing a lamp to splinter into hundreds of pieces. It happens at the only place in the house you forgot to child-proof. Or a youngster comes out of the bathroom rubbing his stomach. "Mommy," he says, "I'll feel real good now. I just ate all of your pills." He had to climb up on the toilet, stand on tiptoes and stretch to a high shelf to reach the container (before the era of child-proof bottles). The pregnant mommy gathers three children together and rushes to the nearest emergency room.

The problems continue. They are limited only by the active imaginations of your kids. Sometimes in your weakest moment you consider loading all of them into your station wagon, driving to the nearest orphanage and negotiating with the supervisor as to how long she'll keep them. I think Erma Bombeck said, "Insanity is inherited. You get it from your children."

Fortunately, we usually produce children when we are young enough to handle them. But in child raising there are many surprises. For example, Abraham, 100 years old, and Sarah, his wife, age 90, living in Old Testament times, became the happy parents of little Isaac. It's a good thing formal education hadn't been invented yet. Imagine the parents at high school graduation, both over 100 years old, as smiling Isaac walks across the stage.

A couple of warnings might help new parents. Realize that not all testing goes on in school. Subtle testing occurs between you and your kids every day. They want to know where the boundaries are. In other words, what can they get away with? At what point do they take you over the edge? This testing begins about the time they start to walk and goes on in one form or another for a lifetime. Peter Ustinov observed that, "Parents are the bones on which children sharpen their teeth."

Further advice for parents: Be aware that in families with multiple children, the kids are born with perfect built-in memories. They can tell you exactly when the allowance for an older brother was raised from $1.25 to $1.75 per week or when the bedtime of an older sister changed from 10:00 to 10:30 p.m. Don't argue these minor points with your youngsters. You'll lose every time, especially because the older children support the memories of the younger ones.

My suggestion to young parents is to keep a scrapbook for each of their children, placing in it not only kindergarten pictures, but also the precious things said. For example, at age four, Phebe prayed, "Dear Jesus, please heal my chicken 'pops.' I still have some. You didn't get all of them." At age six, she questioned me in this manner: "Daddy, if we had 100 people in this house, would we have to sell someone?"

May you, on most days, find it within yourself to believe your little ones are a gift from God.

Daughters Always in Hot Water

At the time I fathered five daughters, I never realized that my own private population explosion would eventually lead to bathroom problems in my middle age.

The ritual of baths, shampoos and hair drying starts at 5:40 a.m. This is so everyone gets an equal chance at the hot water—everyone, that is, except me. Showers for five daughters draw heavily on my 75 gallons of hot water, as well as on my patience.

One of the great battles of the bathroom focuses on the issue of how long a person—each of my daughters, for example—should stand under the shower. Listen as I plead with one of them:

Me: "You don't need to take a 20-minute shower. Any kid should be able to come clean in five minutes."

Daughter: "Hey, I got up at 6:40 a.m. so I wouldn't have to take a five-minute shower. Now go back to bed."

Not only excessive water bills plague me. Staggering electric bills also join in the plot to catapult me into instant bankruptcy. Each hair on each head must be washed and dried each day. This brings in the blow dryer, the curse of our modern day. Blow dryers clutter our bathroom floor, sink and toilet tank. Electric cords, like the tentacles of an octopus, point in every direction, co-mingling with my electric shaver cord and the girls' cords to electric curlers, a sunlamp, a contact lens cleaner and several electric toothbrushes.

One morning l cranked up my courage and went to the basement. The hands on the electric and water meters were spinning furiously like pinwheels on the Fourth of July.

"At least," said my wife, "we're getting dividends from our Dayton Power & Light stock."

"No we're not," I moaned. "I had to sell it to pay the last DP&L bill."

Later, I had a no-win argument with one of the "Finicky Five."

"I've heard that blow dryers have asbestos in them that can cause cancer. Sounds like you should stop using them."

"That's no problem," she said. "We threw out all of the old ones. Just last week we replaced them with new ones that are safe. They'll be on your charge next month."

A strange thing happened a few mornings later. My wife woke me with what she called "good news." "Honey, Martha only took a 15-minute shower. If you hurry, you can take a five-minute shower between her and Rebecca."

Without turning on a light, I jumped out of bed and rushed toward the door. Halfway across the room, I let out a bloodcurdling yell. I had forgotten that my wife had rearranged the furniture the day before. Limping toward the basement door, with the lump on my shin starting to grow, I made a strong executive decision. Only one question remained: Which should I do first—pull the fuse from the fuse box or drain the hot water heater?

Use of Family Telephone Should Be by License Only

You would think that someone smart enough to invent the telephone could have foreseen that it would one day lead to a class struggle in families—those in possession of the phone, sometimes referred to as "teenagers," and those out of possession, sometimes referred to as "suffering parents."

From its inception, the telephone was destined to handle trivia as well as important messages. The first words to be uttered on the marvelous new device on March 10, 1876, were, "Mr. Watson, come here. I want you." (Bell had just spilled some acid on his clothes.) By comparison, remember Samuel F.B. Morse's first telegraphic message on May 24, 1844: "What hath God wrought!" (See Numbers 23:23).

Long distance in the old days was used most sparingly. A long distance call was ordinarily a harbinger of bad news, bringing forth a hush over all occupants in the room. It often signaled a death in the family or some other emergency.

Now long-distance calling has become commonplace. It is used extensively at the drop of your teenager's finger. If you don't believe me, take a look at last month's telephonc bill. After surveying a recent bill I summoned my 16-year-old.

"Why did you call Los Angeles and talk for 45 minutes?" I groaned.

"Oh," she said, "I was just thinking about Nancy, so I called her to ask what she was doing."

I strongly suspect that future bills may reflect telephone forays to distant area codes such as Alaska (907) and Hawaii (808). In many cases 11-digit direct dial telephone calls take the place of letter writing, which has become a lost art for many of our young folks.

But how to hang onto the telephone and still avoid financial ruin is only part of the dilemma facing parents. The greatest problem today is how to get your turn on the phone or, as politicians describe it, "equal time." Have you ever tried calling home from

5

The time has come for children to be licensed
to use the telephone.

the office between 4:00 and 6:00 p.m.?

Teenagers also drape themselves in all positions over the furniture and carpet as they talk. It is discouraging because it looks as if they will be there until the end of the age.

Until now a parent could track the long cord on a telephone and find the teenager at the other end. Then through sign language—and with luck—the importance of your own call could be communicated to the loquacious teenager and you might get possession. But the cordless phone has sprung new problems on us. Now one must look from room to room to find the offending teenager. Recently I discovered that a daughter had barricaded herself in the bathroom and was soaking in the tub while conversing on the cordless.

The time has come for children to be licensed to use the telephone, the same as they are to drive a car. Licensing would involve a course of study, including family finances and common courtesy. Violation of family telephone rules would result in fines, suspension of the license and, in extreme cases, imprisonment.

Good luck, suffering parent, as you spar for possession of your phone.

Being Fruitful and Multiplying

My wife and I took seriously that passage in scripture that said "Be fruitful and multiply." (Genesis 1:22) With seven children, we had been "fruitful," but some of the kids, we found, couldn't multiply. Mathematics was always a problem. One of them argued until the end of a class (and threatened to sue the teacher) claiming that 2 and 2 could be 22 as well as 4. Another was discouraged because the value of "x" kept changing. One graduated (barely) never knowing that pi was 3.14 and why it was in the math room rather than the Home Ec room.

Further, I was not surprised that a Gallup survey disclosed that one out of five of our young folks couldn't find the U.S. on a world map. This squared with my own experience. One of my youngsters (names, ages, sex and IQ of my kids is withheld at their request) thought the Miami River ran through Miami, Florida. Another thought Las Vegas was in California. Yet a third, in trying to match columns, thought that Old Faithful was George Washington.

I looked with envy at bumper stickers proclaiming "My child is an honor student at ABC School." To be perfectly honest, if I had a bumper sticker, it would read, "My kid got through XYZ School by the skin of the teeth."

In fact, all seven kids were dedicated to the proposition that the 3 R's were Readin', Rasslin' and Recess!

I wondered if my flock was deficient in other areas of learning—for example, in physics. I took one of them into the bathroom and flushed the toilet.

Me: Which way does the water go down?
Kid: This way, (circling a finger in air).
Me: Yes, that's counterclockwise—the opposite way the hands of a clock go around.
Kid: Oh!
Me: What direction would a toilet flush in Brazil?
Kid: I didn't know they had plumbing out there. (I strongly suspected the youngster thought Brazil was one of the western states.)
Me: You'll find that south of the equator water swirls, rotates and flushes in the opposite direction or clockwise.
Kid: Impossible!

Within the next month, the young one obtained the address of a cruise ship sailing to South America and wrote to the captain, asking him to flush the toilet 100 miles north of the equator and 100 miles south of the equator and to report the results. The captain was also requested to "park" right on the equator, perform the same experiment and advise. Not having heard from the captain within two weeks, the child found addresses for Chambers of Commerce and foreign tourist information bureaus in South America and New Zealand and popped the same question to several of them.

Two typed letters came from New Zealand. Murray Chapman of the Auckland Chamber of Commerce reported, "The water down here at the bottom of the world flushes clockwise into the toilet." Karina Montgomery from the New Zealand Tourism Department at Wellington wrote, "No one in our section was 100 percent sure if it was anti-clockwise or clockwise and so I put it to the test. Water draining from a sink or toilet in New Zealand will move in a clockwise spin." She went on to say that one of the "chaps" at work checked in the *Encyclopedia Britannica* under "motion" where it states that "the Northern Hemisphere is affected by an anti-clockwise or counterclockwise motion and the Southern Hemisphere is affected by a clockwise motion."

The most encouraging part was when the child came to me and said, "You re right." I'm not sure if the child was launched on a career in engineering, physics or plumbing, but learning was taking place—if only on a bathroom level.

Tasty Crayons Become Hot Commodity in Classroom

For a long time I suspected that "Johnny couldn't read." But never, in my wildest imagination, would I have guessed that Johnny might also be eating crayons in school.

Binney and Smith, manufacturers of Crayola crayons for 53 years, added food scents to their crayons in July, 1994. Recently they announced that their food scents were being changed to "fun scents." Claiming their nontoxic crayons were perfectly safe, the change was made, nevertheless, because of the parents' perception that kids would be tempted to eat crayons.

Never, in my wildest imagination, would I have guessed that Johnny might be eating crayons in school.

Teacher:	"Johnny, why isn't your drawing colored?"
Johnny:	"I don't have any crayons."
Teacher:	"What happened to them?"
Johnny:	"She ate them," pointing to his tablemate, a freckle-faced, pigtailed, gum-chewing girl with a mischievous look and color marks on her lips and chin.

As a further distraction in the classroom, the teacher might have to deal with brisk crayon trading just as kids trade baseball cards: "I'll give you two coconuts (white) for one licorice (black)."

In changing from food scents to fun scents, Binney and Smith created the following new flavors: the color white went from coconut to baby powder, black from licorice to leather jacket, sepia from chocolate to dirt, mahogany from cherry to cedar chest, blue from blueberry to new-car, apricot from peach to lumber, carnation pink from bubble gum to shampoo, yellow from lemon to daffodil and wisteria from grape to lilac.

Binney and Smith state that their scented crayons contain microencapsulated fragrances that release scents only when the crayon is used. The crayons themselves don't smell, but the drawings do.

While Binney and Smith claim their scented crayons are harmless, even if ingested, Dr. Howard Mofenson, Medical Director of The Long Island Regional Poison Control Center, disagrees. He says, "Although the new crayons are marketed as nontoxic and look identical to Crayolas' regular crayons, in actuality they may present an aspiration hazard to small children if placed in their mouths."

However, some families may have adjusted to food-scented crayons in a positive way. How about the kid expecting her snack after school? A note on the kitchen table reads, "Karen, I'm at the mall. I left a few or your favorite crayons in the fridge. Love, Mom."

In spite of Binney and Smith's disclaimer of harm, anything placed in the mouth can become addictive. Thus, a group known as CCA (Crayon Chewers Anonymous) might form in major cities. Scented crayons come in eight packs or sixteen packs. A youngster hooked on eight packs, with a two-pack-a-day habit, could seek professional counseling to kick the habit.

Does the change of scents make sense? Or is it merely nonsense? Problems may still exist.

Mother:	"What's this F in art doing on Ann's report card?"
Teacher:	"Ann is excellent at drawing. Her proportions are good, but she just doesn't have a sense of smell. She mixes scents badly."
Mother:	"I've never heard of such nonsense!"
Teacher:	"Frankly, her work *stinks*!"

Or, picture a young lady climbing into her date's car.

Peggy:	"Bill, your car has a new-car smell."
Bill:	(Surreptitiously popping a Certs in his mouth). "That's impossible. You know this heap is a '75 Buick."

Binney and Smith claim the new scents are the product of focus groups with children. Their groups must have been different from my kids of coloring age who could focus only on recess.

For all elementary school kids: Happy coloring with the new scents, but please don't eat your crayons.

Would You Turn Back If...

It's 4:15 a.m. A light flips on. I am sleeping soundly. I always sleep soundly when I go to bed at 2:15 a.m. and am awakened at 5:30 a.m. But now, a face is coming into view through my blurry eyes. It belongs to my daughter Nancy. Sound waves are hitting the dull nerve endings of my ears: "O.K., get up, you guys. We want to be on the road in an hour."

The family vacation has begun.

12

Space is the biggest problem facing a man with a wife and seven children leaving on vacation. Some of the greatest arguments have revolved around what gets packed and what doesn't. I look over the mound of paraphernalia heaped on the kitchen floor. There is enough stuff to start a sporting goods store, a camera shop and clothing store on Sanibel Island—our destination.

Suddenly, it dawns on me. The only way to pack is to force the family to place everything on the driveway before the first suitcase goes into the trunk. This doesn't make me popular, but it allows me to measure the dimensions of the problem. Using all the art of gentle and some non-gentle persuasion, I encourage the kids to move the mound of cargo onto the driveway. Next, I make a courageous edict.

"This is all that goes, folks. Anything that's not out here now doesn't go to Florida until next year."

Within 20 seconds my daughter Martha comes to the car.

"Dad, I just found your tennis racket, fishing gear and camera in the family room. What shall I do with them?"

I quickly explain to the kids that there are exceptions and footnotes to all rules, especially when I make them.

When leaving on a vacation with multiple children, the bathroom ritual becomes important. In earlier years we demanded that each child visit the bathroom the last thing before being considered roadworthy. Then Mary came up with a new theory. It was that if you can get each child to go twice, you can get twice as much mileage out of him or her. The theory was never fully proved or disproved. However, we had to abandon the practice when we found that some of the kids were getting up early and drinking large quantities of water just so they could make two bathroom visits and get out of the house.

Another ritualistic part of the vacation is the departing family picture. Although I can make the family pose for the picture standing beside the car, I haven't yet learned how to put a smile on their faces this early in the morning.

Then as the car rolls down the driveway, I direct someone to write down the time and mileage. These statistics are duly noted on our AAA triptik. But this is the last we think of them, forgetting to enter the same information as we arrive at Sanibel Island.

We turn down Stroop Road, heading toward I-75. At this time, the kids start a game. It is called "Would You Turn Back If." It goes like this: "Dad, would you turn back if I forgot to pack my sneakers?" This goes on for several miles and forces me to think, which is hard to do under the circumstances. But finally, the game is getting to me and I am forced to tell the kids at this point, "I wouldn't even turn back if we forgot one of you."

However, this conversation reminds me to check my wallet to see if I have all of my credit cards. Fortunately I have them. If they were all laid end to end, they would stretch from the 50-yard line to the end zone on a football field. I can't remember how we traveled before the era of charge cards. I have subscribed, at least in part, to the slogan on travel agency walls: "Play now—pay later."

As we drive onto the bridge to cross the Ohio River, I remember an earlier vacation. I had just told the kids that as soon as we got off the bridge, they'd be in Kentucky. One of the younger ones looked out and claimed it wasn't so. The child had seen Kentucky on the map at school and it was yellow. I thought the kid was getting smarter until the following year when she told me that there was only one state between Ohio and Florida, and that was Kentucky. She was sure because she had seen Kentucky Fried Chicken signs all the way.

With nine of us plus luggage packed into an eight-passenger station wagon, and after a two-day drive, we are miraculously still talking to each other as we wheel onto Sanibel Island.

I'm glad the good Lord provided for childbearing and rearing while we're still young.

FOOD FOR THOUGHT

Gardener's Lament
Springtime gardening's fun
With fresh new packs of seeds.
But show me just one guy
Who likes those August weeds.

Statistics show that the average family spends a substantial amount of time and money per year buying, preparing, eating and digesting food. Additionally, as we consider food-related activities, the hours and costs escalate significantly. Such activities include money spent to lose or redistribute pounds we have already accumulated. Thus, fees for exercise classes, country club expenses and tennis court time claim part of our monthly budget. And even medical, hospital, prescription and dietetic expenses, as well as funeral and burial expenses in some cases, reflect dietary decisions.

John Patterson, founder of NCR, placed pithy sayings on the sides of his buildings. A thought-provoking one proclaimed, "We are a part of all we have met." Passing this building hundreds of times, I wondered what might happen if some rogue changed the sign to read, "We are a part of all we have *et*."

It might at least give pause to those who ingest exotic foods such as snails, octopi, snakes, ostriches, mice, ants and grasshoppers.

Good luck as you make culinary choices with lifetime effects.

That Looks Interesting. Can You Explain It?

Remember your kindergartner popping into the house with a picture from school? He is beaming from ear to ear, proud of his masterpiece. As a parent you are perplexed trying to figure it out. Is it an octopus or a spider? A pumpkin or an orange? A farmer and his wife planting potatoes or Adam and Eve in the Garden of Eden?

Educators tell us we should never ask the little tyke what it is. This can scar him for life, causing rebellion in later years. Antisocial behavior could result, such as robbing banks, or more serious offenses like taking candy from small babies, pushing senior citizens into mud puddles or brushing teeth sideways instead of up and down.

So the proper way to handle your child's picture is to say, "That looks interesting. Can you explain it to me?"

The same caution should be exercised as you sit down to eat dinner. Never, but never, say to the cook: "What is it?" If you're sitting at the table, if it's mealtime and some object is in a dish with steam (or maybe smoke) rising from it, you are no doubt looking at some kind of food. If you can't identify it, simply say, "This looks interesting; can you explain it to me?"

Unfortunately early in our marriage, I looked across the dinner table and bluntly asked, "What is this?" My wife answered, "Asparagus." When I asked where the tips were, she replied that we had eaten them the night before.

For some diners, mealtime becomes a religious experience. Perhaps this is so because they are confronted night after night with a burnt offering. One family I know has agreed, by way of compromise, to say the blessing at the end of the meal so they know just how thankful to be.

The following advice is offered to those on the receiving end of meals:

- Don't grit your teeth and mutter that you'll eat the entree even if it kills you.

Never bring a bag of McDonald's hamburgers to the table.

- Don't pop Tums in your mouth as the meal progresses.
- Never bring a bag of McDonald's hamburgers to the table.
- Never get a tool from the workshop to cut the meat.
- Never call the fire department just because a little smoke drifts in from the kitchen.
- Don't feed the main course to the dog while the cook isn't looking.

It is hoped this advice will bring closer together those who prepare meals and those who eat them, and that indigestion and heartburn will be replaced with a feeling of good will as family members confront the evening meal.

Bon Appetit!

Read My Lips—No More Broccoli

On my scorecard, President Bush was doing everything exactly right. That is, until the last week of March 1990. At that time our beloved president condemned broccoli. He came out of the closet—er, make that pantry—and said, "I do not like broccoli. And I haven't liked it since I was a little kid and my mother made me eat it. I'm president of the United States, and I'm not going to eat any more broccoli."

At once, raising children became a tougher job. For years parents have been challenging children in this manner: "If you study hard and do your sums on a coal shovel in front of the fireplace, if you don't push and shove on the school bus, if you don't run the rocking chair over the cat's tail, if you floss your teeth once a day and if you eat your broccoli (substitute cauliflower, brussels sprouts, lima beans, spinach, etc.), you may grow up to be president some day."

My seven children have all decided *not* to be president and have set their own dietary course, but there are millions of younger kids out there who by now have declared their independence from broccoli and are harder to manage.

A dangerous precedent has been set by President Bush. Thus, another president on another day might viciously attack apple pie or even motherhood or the American flag.

Personally, I have lost faith. I would no longer buy a sack lunch from this president.

But two years are left until the Republican Convention. I hope G.B. will recant and become the *broccoli* president. I want to vote for him in 1992.

Florida Judge Opens a New Can of Peas

A news story in *The Journal Herald* on September 22, 1983, reported that a judge in Florida is requiring defendants to pay fines in food instead of cash. The judge is also extracting food from lawyers as a penalty for being late with filing legal papers. The food is then distributed to needy residents.

I wonder if Fort Lauderdale lawyers are adding No. 10 cans of fruits and vegetables to their supply rooms. Perhaps they are heading to the courthouse with a few cans of spinach in a grocery sack to cover any possible contempt-of-court rulings.

If this catches on across the country, all lawyers should take note. It is certainly food for thought.

Let Them Eat Dandelions

New Yorkers may now rest easier knowing that the dangerous dandelion-napper has been apprehended. The *Journal Herald's*

April 1986 story titled "Please Don't Eat the Daisies" describes how a bespectacled botanist, Steve Brill, was arrested for conducting walking tours of New York City's parks, teaching city dwellers which plants were edible and having them taste samples.

Unfortunately, in Brill's last tour he had signed on two undercover park rangers, who put the bite on him at the end of the tour.

Some of the eaten material was as prolific as the dandelion— a weed. Many of us would like to turn Brill and his entourage loose in our own yards during spring.

Admittedly, Brill probably should have limited his enjoyment of the foliage to touching and smelling. Let's hope that the judge dealing with the case put it in proper perspective, realizing that in New York City—and particularly Central Park—some really heavy crime takes place.

Meanwhile, back in Central Park, don't be surprised if the rangers detain visitors to give saliva tests and look for yellow stains on their fingers and mouths.

McRobot Comes to Aid of McDonald's

I recently found an interesting article in a Fort Myers, Florida, newspaper that stated a six-armed robot is being developed on an experimental basis to run a major hamburger restaurant. It will serve its first hamburger between December and February in Manhattan.

While the robot will be programmed to take orders, prepare and serve food, make change, clear tables and clean up spills, there is no indication that the robot will be able to respond to that all-too-frequent event in the fast-food industry—robbery.

Let us hope the genius who is developing the robot will find some way to make it respond appropriately to the rogue who comes in and orders all of the money from the register rather than six hamburgers to go.

But then seeing six arms raised upon commanding "Stick 'em up" might confound and disarm the felon.

Talking Scales Make Plain "The Battle of the Bulge"

As I wonder where the grocery money goes, I need only turn sideways and look in the mirror. For me, "the battle of the bulge" started at Jack Benny's age. I lose the battle at the dinner table and confirm it later at the bathroom scales.

Recently, I've had trouble telling whether my scales were reading 190 pounds or 180 pounds. This, with or without my glasses. Naturally, I resolved all doubts in favor of the lower poundage. Surely there must be a constitutional presumption in favor of the lesser weight.

But I decided to solve the dilemma by installing "talking scales" in my bathroom. I wasn't sure that talking scales existed, but I was determined to find out.

Thus started a long series of questions to my friends. To the question "Do you know where I may buy talking scales?" most of them shook their heads slowly in disbelief. Some, I'm sure, felt I necded to be probated.

Finally, a friend suggested that I call Hammacher Schlemmer, a department store in New York City. Ordering the talking scales by telephone was as easy as giving my Visa number. The package arrived by UPS within three business days, as promised.

It was a pleasure to finally receive something that didn't need assembly other than inserting two nine-volt batteries. But that didn't mean no decisions had to be made.

First Decision: I must set a switch in the back of the scales to talk in "pounds" or "kilograms." For me the decision was easy;

I'm too old to go metric. (Metric is hectic!) But be advised that metric may sound better than its English equivalent. For example, 201 pounds is only 92 kilograms. The problem is you are just as heavy in either system.

Second Decision: I must select a salutation to be announced by the scales at the end of the weigh-in. The choice, surprisingly, is between "Have a good day" and "Good-bye."

First, let's consider "Have a good day." This is the most absurd cliché in the English language. Further, how can you "Have a good day" if the scales have just announced "You have gained 10 pounds." Additional confusion may ensue if you weigh in at bedtime, instead of first thing in the morning.

Next, let's consider the alternative: "Good-bye." This sounds too final, as if your next weigh-in session might be on that great scales in the sky. I grudgingly opted for "Have a nice day."

Third Decision: My final decision was to pick a PIN (Personal Identification Number) between one and five. You see, the talking scales had memory for five individuals. To keep things simple, I chose number one.

The weighing process starts by thrusting your right big toe into the "on" button. The following conversation ensues:

Scales:	"Enter your identification number." (My left big toe presses number one.)
Me:	"There you are."
Scales:	"Please step on scales."
Me:	"O.K."
Scales:	"Your weight is 190 pounds."
Me:	"Oh no!"
Scales:	"You have gained five pounds." (This means the last weigh-in was 185 pounds.)
Me:	"Impossible."
Scales:	"Have a nice day."

Of course, you don't need to talk back to your scales, but it does make you feel like you're involved in the process and more important than a mere number.

Whoever said, "Talk is cheap" was not referring to talking scales. But it was worth one-tenth of my monthly Social Security check to know my precise weight and to have something to talk to around the house. And it seems like a frugal investment when I compute (based on Life Expectancy Tables) that I can weigh in daily 4,380 more times.

I wonder what will happen when its batteries run down. With less power will I be the beneficiary of less weight? Or might the voice blurt out my weight in a descending discord, as when the plug is pulled on an old-fashioned record player? Eventually, I'll need to return my marvelous machine to the manufacturer for repairs with a note stating, "Its voice is gone."

Before you order your talking scales, you should know that at 288 pounds it will max out, with the voice announcing "overload." And to prevent damage, the instructions inform, "Do not weigh more than 300 pounds."

Have fun with your talking scales!

Banana Story Stirs Bunch of *Fuelish* Possibilities

While vacationing in Florida, I saw an article in the Fort Myers paper indicating that bananas may be used as a source of power for automobiles in the future.

Although banana power may not have *a-peel* for everyone, if it ever catches on, it will revolutionize our traveling habits.

Road signs on the expressways will no doubt read "Next Exit: Food—Lodging—Bananas." Listen as your wife says, "Honey, you had better exit here. Your banana gauge shows you're almost on empty." And what of the poor guy who runs out of bananas? You can spot him a mile away as he trudges back to his stranded car on the expressway carrying a large bunch of bananas on his shoulder.

Instead of the customary gas station, picture your friendly

Your banana gauge shows you're on empty.

neighborhood fruit stand with three grades of bananas advertised: regular, unpeeled and super unpeeled. While filling up, the courteous attendant will also check your banana oil.

No doubt credit cards will be issued by Chiquita, Dole, Delmonte and other major banana producers. These cards will provide fuel for travel all over the country and might even buy a banana split at the dairy bar.

The idle chatter at the office will now center on how many miles per bunch instead of per gallon. And if bananas should ever become scarce, the "banana hog" will be the object of the same scorn as today's "gas hog."

Banana fuel will also have worldwide implications. Obviously, the oil-producing countries will become poor second-class nations, while the prestige of the banana republics will be greatly enhanced. Can you visualize representatives of the Central and South American countries sitting around a table at the First Banana Summit presided over by the Top Banana? They are trying to agree on the price hike for a bunch of bananas.

It's downright frightening, isn't it?

III

DANGLING PARTICIPLES AND OTHER SERIOUS LANGUAGE PROBLEMS

Error Conditioned
I love to find error.
It's right down my line.
I hotly pursue it.
Except when it's mine.

For years I corrected a secretary, Linda, on a matter of grammar. Whenever she said bad, as in "I feel *bad*," I said, "No, you feel *badly*." Apparently I wasn't paying attention back in the 30s and 40s when I was in school. She reasoned, "You wouldn't say 'goodly' would you?" By the time she learned that she had been correct for 20 years, fortunately, I had retired. Linda has been very nice about it, despite the *few hundred* times she has mentioned it to me. Essentially it was a good learning experience for me. Be careful about corrections because as sure as you point out your friend's error, you'll come up with a whopper yourself.

My boyhood family had a bank on the dining room table. Fines were assessed against parents and children for improper English. No, this neither destroyed conversation nor gave us indigestion. When the bank was full, we went to the ice cream store for milk shakes and chocolate sundaes, thus proving that improper English, properly handled, can actually be fattening. I recommend the good English bank on your table in spite of its risk of extra calories.

In my own family, the good English bank didn't go over. Frankly, the kids outnumbered us and voted it out. But as an alternative, we turned to Roz Young to arbitrate grammar problems. Roz is indisputably the Dean of the English language in the Miami Valley and beyond. I have learned many interesting things from her. For example, did you know it is not incorrect to end a sentence with a preposition? By mutual agreement, family members have always agreed to abide by Roz' decisions. Likewise, in disputes in the workplace or elsewhere, Roz' word is final.

But something has always bothered me. Who is there? Is it *I* or is it *me*? In other words, what is the state of health of the predicate nominative? Roz wrote that the rule as we learned it in the old days is "gone with the wind," like most of the teachers who taught it. The battle is lost as colloquialisms come to the front. Roz recommended an excellent book. It is *Webster's Dictionary of English Usage*. Likewise, I would recommend it to you.

Since placing hieroglyphics on cave walls in prehistoric times, man has continually tried to communicate with unknown future inhabitants of the earth. Thus, as the remains of an author lie in the grave, his or her writings may delight readers for many years thereafter. Consider, for example, the works of Shakespeare, Mark Twain and Hemingway.

I must confess, I hope this book will have a life beyond this body. Perhaps my great grandchildren and their grandchildren will enjoy it in the next millennium. Indeed, I hope my descendant, a young boy in the 21st Century, will climb to the attic some rainy afternoon, locate my book, blow the dust from it and then downstairs ask his parents, "Who is this guy, Tom Cecil? What's he trying to say, and am I related to him some way?"

What can you or I do to preserve this beautiful heritage known as the English language? I decided to form a language police group known as NAG (Nitpickers At Grammar). Modestly, I named myself president. Slots are still open for vice-president, treasurer, secretary and board members. NAG will identify errors in newspapers, magazines, books, advertisements, radio and television. A NAG member will then send a constructive note of criticism to the writer or speaker, pointing out the offensive language.

I hope you will take good care of this precious heritage of the English language, whether you are writing "the great American novel," a letter to a college student, a valentine for a special person, a guest column for the newspaper, or a "stick-up" note at your friendly neighborhood bank.

Let's get busy now before colloquialisms, clichés, split infinitives and dangling participles overrun us.

Watch Close—Make that Closely—For All Those Pesky Adverbs

I woke up in a cold sweat a few nights ago. It was 3:00 a.m. The problem was adverbs—their use and abuse. This has troubled me for about 50 years.

I had this nagging feeling that the traffic warning signs reading "slow" should actually read "slowly." If a driver were charged with speeding on Far Hills Avenue, it might work out like this:

Judge: "How do you plead?"

Driver: "Not guilty, sir."

Judge: "Did you see the 'slow' sign?"

Driver: "Yes, but I didn't think it involved me."

Judge: "What is your plea based on?"

Driver: "Improper English, sir. 'Slow' is an adjective. I would only reduce speed for a 'slowly' sign."

Judge: "Bailiff, this man belongs in an institution. Take him out of here quick."

Bailiff: "Do you mean *quickly*, sir?"

Judge: "Thirty days for both of you!"

Adverb abuse is everywhere. Look at the used-car ads in your daily paper. Several of them say "Runs good." Would you buy a used car from someone who writes like that? Could you trust such a person? Of course not! Poor English is a progressive thing. Adverb abuse today; tomorrow, split infinitives or dangled participles. Don't encourage these people by buying their cars.

The ceiling of my dentist's office has a poster of a sleeping lion on it. It's not that I go around with my head cocked at an angle, watching ceilings. However, as the dental hygienist tilts the

Would you buy a used car from a dealer who advertises
"Runs good?"

chair and cleans my teeth, this bruiser of an animal comes into view. The caption says: "I wake up slow." I hope my dentist reads this and adds "ly" to his poster before my next appointment.

But, education also should be practical. The point is, if you are walking through the woods and come across one of these sleeping critters, I suggest you put a lot of distance between him and you. Then sit down on a stump and figure out whether he'll wake up "slow" or "slowly."

I don't want to come across as a pedantic. I have made my share of errors with adverbs as well as other parts of speech. In fact, my first experience with adverbs was bad. In grade school, the teacher explained that adverbs end in "ly" and asked us to write a page full. I finished the assignment in 15 seconds, wondering why the other students were still writing.

The teacher invited me to stand up and read my list. Trembling, I stood and read "fly" and "sly."

Once my English teacher returned a theme to me marked "D-minus." I marched to her desk and asked for an explanation. She said I had dangled several participles. I agreed that I had, but told her I thought I hadn't dangled them too far. She had no sense of humor and the bad grade stuck. But, on the positive side, I decided to try harder with grammar and writing.

My observation is that proper speech is not emphasized enough or considered as relevant as it was when I was in school.

Heard too often at your neighborhood school: "Me and him are going to the mall after school." Students walk down the hall destroying not school property but the King's English.

A joke in a recent *Reader's Digest* says it better than I:

"Jill," a teacher reprimanded the teenager in the hall, "do you mind telling me whose class you're cutting this time?"

"Well," the young woman explained, "see, OK, like it's like I really don't like think like that's really important y' know, like because I'm y' know, like I don't get anything out of it."

"It's Mrs. Winthrop's English class, isn't it?" the teacher replied.

Rudolf Flesch wrote the book *Why Johnny Can't Read*. Once we figure out why Johnny can't read, we might then discover why he can't adequately write, speak or spell either. But poor English is not to be laid only on the doorstep of our youth. Conceivably an octogenarian could split an infinitive on his death bed. Surely he would be held accountable for it though.

But, the importance of proper usage must be drilled into our students starting at an early age.

I once had the easy job of selecting a secretary from two young women who responded on the telephone. One said: "I seen your ad in the paper." The other answered, when I asked for Karen, "This is she."

NAG (Nitpickers at Grammar) is described on page 27. Vacancies are still open for officers and a Board of Directors. I hope you will apply, but you must respond quick—er, quickly.

Clichés: An Airborne Verbal Communicable Disease

Warning: the following column discusses a verbal communicable disease in frank and adult terms. If you feel you would be offended by reading this, please stop immediately.

I vowed if I heard one more person say, "at this point in time," I would take strong action. "At this point in time" means "now"; "at that point in time" means "then." Why can't people simply say "now" and "then"? The person who uses the offensive phrase will no doubt recognize himself or herself in reading this column and desist at once.

I started on my crusade to correct this verbal communicable disease by calling Roz Young, whom I consider to be *the* authority in the Miami Valley. Roz says the phrase started with John Dean at the time of the Watergate hearings, and that while Dean was saying "at this point in time," he was framing the answer to the question then being asked of him. Almost 20 years later, it is still with us.

The phrase is known as a cliché. The *Random House Dictionary* defines a cliché as "a trite, stereotyped expression; a sentence or phrase, usually expressing a popular or common thought or idea, that has lost originality, ingenuity, and impact by long overuse, as *sadder but wiser*, or *strong as an ox*."

The word "cliché" comes from the French. I wish they had never invented it. Picture two Frenchmen at a sidewalk café in Paris:

First Frenchman:	"Let's invent some kind of curse to put on the English language."
Second Frenchman:	"Yes! Let's put clichés in their language!"
First Frenchman:	"It will drive them crazy."

Coming back to my warning at the beginning of this column, I firmly believe that clichés are a "communicable verbal disease" often becoming airborne and spreading quickly by words—either verbal or written. Our air is fouled not only by pollutants, but also by clichés, from New York to California and from Minnesota to Texas. They cut across all facets of our daily lives.

For example, in politics consider "jump start the economy," "sound bite," "photo opportunity," "post-convention bump," "spin doctors," "spending caps," "the president defined himself," "grow the economy," "no free lunch," "empowerment," "politically correct," and "a third way." "Read my lips" is in a category of its own and reminds us that candidates may get in trouble if the cliché is in the form of a promise broadcast to millions of Americans.

In sports we have "slam dunk," "fluke," "overachiever," "give 110%" and "put some points on the scoreboard." Where else would you put them?

Why must Willard Scott on *The Today Show* say "Here's what's happening in your area *even as we speak*," which simply means "now" or perhaps "right now." And why must other weather persons say "shower activity" instead of rain?

Clichés often have a long life. Some, in fact, relate back to the book of Proverbs in the Bible. William Safire, in a column about language, reminds us that "the earth moved" wasn't a cliché when Ernest Hemingway coined it in 1940 and that "making a mountain of a molehill" dates back to the 1500s.

My suggestion to writers and speakers is to avoid clichés like the plague. Whoops! Make that "avoid them *vigorously*." It is better to eliminate clichés and use your own imagination as you write and speak. Also a computer program known as *Grammatik IV* will spot clichés and other writing problems for you.

But there is a positive side to clichés. James Rogers has compiled a *Dictionary of Clichés* describing meanings and origins of over 2,000 entries. In his introduction Rogers says, "Among people who do pay attention to their phrasing, however, clichés can serve as the lubricant of language: summing up a point or a situation, easing a transition in thought, adding a seasoning of humor to a discourse." George Will, Rogers points out, took "through thick and thin," and wrote that the avid Chicago Cubs' fans support their team through "thin and thin."

Perhaps there is a word or cliché that irritates you as much as fingers dragging across a blackboard. If so, relief is at hand. Send the offensive word or words to Lake Superior State University, Sault Saint Marie, MI 49783. This school, as a gimmick to get on the map, has been compiling a list of useless and overused words since 1976, releasing annual recommendations on those it feels should be banished from the English language. Entries received by November 30 will be considered for the current year. Those received after that date will be considered for the next year. Publication of the *All Time Dishonor List of Words Banished from the Queen's English* follows in January.

About clichés, I'd like to strike a compromise with you. I won't say, "Have a nice day" if you won't say "at this point in time."

Processed Tree Carcasses? Surely Not!

The thermometer outside reads five below zero. As the doors of the elevator close, another passenger remarks to you, "Wow, it's meteorologically challenging out there!" Don't worry, the fellow is harmless, but he is speaking a strange new language known as political correctness.

Thus a newspaper is said to come from a processed tree carcass. At least so say the language police who study and report "politically correct" (PC) writing and speech. In the same category as your newspaper are books, magazines and paper bags.

Here are some more examples of PC language. The PC phrase comes first, with the traditional word in parentheses: hair disadvantaged (bald), cerebrally challenged (stupid), batchild (batboy), nontraditional shopper (looter), terminally inconvenienced (dead), negative saver (spendthrift), vehicle appearance specialist (car washer), electorally slighted (defeated). I'm sure George Bush will be glad to know that he was "electorally slighted" rather than defeated. Still other examples: stolen products (eggs, milk, cheese, honey and wool), animal companion (pet), snowperson (snowman), and motivationally possessed (lazy).

Using PC as a speech standard causes unintended slurs. Politicians especially seem to put their foot (instead of PC) in their mouth. For example, the White House has apologized to people of Welsh heritage for President Clinton's use of the expression "*welsh* on your debts." And the president again ran afoul of PC standards when he predicted that the '96 campaign would be "a fight to the *finish*." Finally, the wrath of Holland was felt when the president explained that when he and Hillary ate at college, they went *dutch*.

Colin Powell opened a can of worms when he disclaimed that he was a presidential candidate. He said, "It's time to *scotch* the rumors." Meanwhile, back in Georgia, Phil Gramm's presidential campaign ran into trouble when he asked for "a cup of coffee and *danish* to go." Gramm never understood what all the fuss was about and said, "It was all *Greek* to me."

Other applications of PC produce bizarre results. Consider the following:

- Sensitivity police cracked down on Alex Longo, a New Jersey first-grader who showed up at school with birthday invitations for nine boys in his class. Since no girls were on the list, his teacher said it violated school policies of gender-equity and inclusion. She sent him home with the invitations. The boy's dad wondered whether all future pajama parties would have to be half male.

- In response to complaints that "SLOW CHILDREN" traffic signs are insensitive to retarded youngsters, the state of Massachusetts wants towns to change to "WATCH CHILDREN" signs.

- A British professor wrote to the *Times* of London complaining that PC people had deleted the reference to Parson Brown performing a wedding in the song *Winter Wonderland*. He wondered whether musical references to marriage offend the "sacramentally challenged."

- Ann Landers wrote a column recently about the problems of extremely thin women, whom she described as looking "consumptive." After some thin women wrote in to complain, Ann pleaded guilty to insensitivity.

- Political correctness has invaded space! NASA has buckled under fussbudget accusations that Buck Rogers' terminology is sexist. As a result, NASA will no longer refer to "manned" flights but will describe the missions as "habitated" and "unhabitated," or "crewed" and "uncrewed." Says a NASA spokesman: "We have been ordered to delete any reference by sex on the grounds that 'manned' flight is crude." Female astronauts find these linguistic aerobics foolish. Says one, "Common sense is the victim of all this rhetoric."

- *The New Testament and Psalms: An Inclusive Version* (Oxford University Press) was the PC biblical make-over of the year. Note these changes: The Lord's Prayer now begins, "Our Father-Mother in heaven." The 63rd Psalm's "Thy right hand upholds me" made lefthanders feel bad and is now "your strong hand upholds me." "Kingdom," an overly male word, is now "dominion."

- In the Stanford Memorial Church, religiously inclined freshmen may be surprised to find that Bibles have been removed. The church staff has deemed the books exclusionary toward people of other faiths.

- We were dismayed to discover several things when re-reading Clement Clarke Moore's classic *A Visit from St. Nicholas*. Only the man of the house springs from his bed to see "what was the matter." The missus passively stays put, while the children dream of empty-calorie, sugarplum candy. St. Nicholas comes down the chimney of a woodburning fireplace that pollutes the air. Not only is he "dressed all in fur"; he also smokes a pipe, is obese and florid, suggesting high blood pressure.

- Donna Ellen Cooperman carried PC to ridiculous heights. Fighting her way through the New York court system, she was permitted to change her name to *Donna Ellen Cooperperson*.

Acceptance of PC speech at 100 percent will cause problems. In almost every situation, the PC terminology is several words longer than the word or words it attempts to replace. For example, a "riot" has been defined as a "spontaneous display of community dissatisfaction with prevailing socioeconomic conditions." Obviously

PC speech causes more, not less use of "processed tree carcasses" as longer newspapers, books and magazines roll off the presses. Additionally, any after-dinner speech—already a consummate bore—will become longer, putting audiences to sleep sooner.

Communication will become more difficult between a straight talker and a PC-er, with the latter having to explain his erudite language in plain English. In fact, I suggest that PC advocates be assigned their own area—perhaps the states of Idaho, Montana, Utah and Wyoming.

I predict utter confusion as PC-ers try to reform French, Latin and other languages in which nouns are designated as male or female. Good luck!

While some of the definitions are relevant to the '90s and are important, I will not be speaking PC speech for the most part. I have always "called a spade a spade." But then, maybe I should redefine it as an "implement for removing dirt."

Material for this column was gleaned from *The Official Politically Correct Dictionary and Handbook* by Harry Beard and Christopher Cerf, and the following periodicals: *Time* magazine, *U.S. News & World Report*, *Fortune* magazine, *The New Yorker* magazine, *National Review* magazine and *Vegetarian News*.

Teacher's Promise Gives New Meaning to the Word "Bookworm"

Johnny's failure to read (*Why Johnny Can't Read* by Rudolf Flesch) could be linked to his teacher's failure to eat worms in front of his class.

Shirley DiRado, a Los Angeles school principal, promised to eat a worm if each student at her school read at least two books during a project known a "Reading is FUNdamental." Making good on her promise, DiRado ate two worms instead of one in front of

Will future worm-eating events become the subject of
negotiations between students and teachers?

an assembly of several hundred youngsters, ages 6 to 11. The two worms were swished down with orange juice.

Said DiRado after the culinary fete, "It wasn't something I liked doing, certainly not my favorite food, but it was a promise I made and I wanted to show the children that promises are made to be kept."

Meanwhile, an elementary school teacher in Belding, Michigan, brought off a similar worm performance. Chuck Matlock's pledge was to eat four worms if his 232 kids would read 7,000 books during March, National Reading Month. Spurred on by the gruesome offer, the students read 7,785 books. Matlock gulped down four worms boiled in lemon juice and salt. Stretching the demonstration for all it was worth, he claimed, "Really, worms have as much protein as a t-bone steak without gristle." He said he was ready to challenge the students again next year, especially if the principal, Judy Feuerstein, would join in.

Several questions arise:

Will students only agree to become bookworms if their teachers and professors eat worms?

Will college students pursuing a degree in education be required to take "Worms 103"?

Can worm-eating teachers of English and reading receive additional compensation for their heroic efforts?

Might this reading tool be used by teachers in the Miami Valley?

How long will it be before animal rights activists protest and picket the offending schools?

How long will it be until the Secretary of Agriculture and the F.D.A. start an investigation?

Will future worm-eating events become the subject of negotiations between students and teachers to determine how many worms the teacher will eat and how many books the students will read?

This is only a worms-eye-view of such a project in two schools. Let's hope that Johnnys and Janes in other school districts might get hooked on books for other reasons. There must be a better way for educators to *worm* their way into students' hearts.

IV

SPORTS, EXERCISE AND OTHER BAD HABITS

Athlete's Foot
The runner with his feet so fleet
Runs each morning down my street.
No runner I, I'll lie in bed
And let him get sore feet instead.

Usually your kids get started on sports at an early stage. For example, Junior is sitting in his high chair and propels his spinach at a nearby wall. He then turns, grinning, and looks at you for some kind of reaction. You should never offer any signs of approval or encouragement.

Or your daughter in her high chair, without any prior notice, suddenly flips her bowl of pablum upside down and onto the floor. She is trying to make a statement. The statement is: I'm not in a pablum mood this morning.

But back to the spinach thrower. He will eventually learn how to load up the business end of a spoon with spinach and, using the left forefinger and his right thumb and forefinger, as well as the spoon, he will make a missile of the spinach. As it hits the wall and runs down, he grins in delight. A youngster who reaches this stage is probably too old to be in a high chair. As a matter of fact, some kids still do this missile stunt at college.

Also be on the lookout for the youngster who has lost one of her front teeth. Invariably during the prayer before meals, she'll load up on water and shoot a perfect stream on her little brother across the table. Usually the blessing ends at this point. She is also skillful enough to hit a fly crawling on the wall from halfway across the room.

You should realize that as your kids go through these stages, they are starting to develop valuable hand-eye coordination skills that will help them in real sports in the future.

Since I oppose unnecessary walking, I naturally resist all forms of running—unless someone is chasing me.

As your youngster develops, he'll also play hide and seek with you. He *hides* your valuables—wallet, watch, car keys—and you *seek* them. Kids love to squirrel things away.

As children develop, they become more sociable and learn to play games together. Indeed, at an early age, I was reprimanded by my parents for hitting my sister, Nancy, over the head with the Uncle Wiggly board.

Sports become more physical as your child grows older. Most of them next go through the kick-the-can and red-rover stage. The latter game sometimes produces victims when the neighborhood tough guy tries to crash through the line. Broken arms and dislocated shoulders end up in the office of your friendly neighborhood orthopedic doctor. But then someone needs to keep them busy!

Moving right along, we come to sports played in schools. Baseball was never my forte. As the two captains formed their teams, I was always the last to be chosen. It was as if I was thrown in for good luck rather than as a serious player. We also played football after school. I caught the ball once and ran for the goal. I looked around and, to my amazement, the fellows chasing me and yelling at me were my *own* teammates, whom I thought were my friends. I was scared, and the faster they ran, the more spirited became my drive for the goal. As you no doubt have guessed, I was running in the wrong direction and made a touchdown for the other team. After this, I was known as "Wrong Way Cecil." This phrase originated with a young Irish pilot by the name of Corrigan. He filed his flight plan for a cross-country flight from New York to California but ended up in Ireland, claiming that he got lost. He was known thereafter as "Wrong Way Corrigan."

I hope you are enjoying some appropriate sport for your age. Whether it's checkers or shuffleboard or something in between, *have fun*.

Avoid Unnecessary Walking at All Cost

Of the thousands of four-letter verbs in our English language, my least favorite is the word "walk." I have tried to avoid unnecessary walking at all costs, reasoning that if the Lord had really wanted me to walk, I would have been born with shoes.

Thus, it is not unusual for me to hop in my car or riding lawn mower and motor to our next-door neighbor's house to borrow a tool or deliver a missent letter. After the initial shock, my neighbors now think nothing of it.

Mine is the car you see with the motor running, parked in the fire lane in front of the cleaners or idling in the bus zone at Third and Main, as I dash to a deposit slot at the savings and loan.

I have attempted to go on shopping ventures with my wife and daughters at the mall (another four-letter word). They dash madly from store to store, sniffing out bargains, holding up merchandise, "oohing" and "aahing" and occasionally trying something on. They can knock over three dozen stores in an hour's time. Early on, my feet resisted this, and I designated a bench where I met my shoppers when the stores closed. From this restful haven, I people-watched, read or wrote.

Since I oppose unnecessary walking, I naturally resist all forms of running—unless someone is chasing me. I subscribe to Red Skelton's philosophy on jogging. "I do not jog," he said. "I get all my exercise as a pallbearer for my friends who did."

The Big One That Got Away

Is there anything better than a day on the lake? The summer breeze blows gently over my face; the waves lap soothingly against my boat; the seat grows harder every minute; my non-backlash reel puts inextricable knots in my line; and then there is the ever-present prospect of catching a bass, a bluegill, or another hunk of seaweed.

For years I have fished streams, lakes, rivers and oceans, catching thousands of mosquito bites, colds, sunburns and bad tempers.

The average layman thinks the only bad luck in connection with fishing is going home with an empty stringer. But my misfortune starts just as soon as I go to the attic in search of my tackle box. Finding the contents of my box is even more complicated.

For example, my son's kite usually has about 100 yards of my 20-pound test line—that is, if the kite did not get away from him in a strong wind or if my wife did not find the line before he did and use it for wrapping packages. While being questioned about my fishing gear, my son usually breaks down and confesses that he has melted all of my lead weights in his molding set and that my rod is down in Johnny's basement where the gang used it to practice fencing. About the same time, my oldest daughter admits she has taken the three-pronged hooks out of my favorite plugs and used the plugs for floating toys while bathing her youngest sister in the bathtub.

Once at the lake, I visit the bait shack, a common sight at all the lakes I have frequented. To stimulate my interest in fishing, the walls of the bait shop are bedecked with a dozen varieties of mounted fish. But I am not fooled by them. They are only decoys which have been imported from Canada or Alaska.

Standard equipment at one of these shacks is an old codger who has that smug, unconcerned look that seems to say he has caught so many fish in his lifetime that it would bore him to even say the word "fish" and that the sight of a hearty bass would actually make him sick.

Sometimes, though, this old disciple of Isaac Walton will divulge important advice, especially if I prod him gently with the end of my pole. He will peek out from under his straw hat just long enough to tell me that I have come at the wrong time.

"Last week they were jumping into the boats after the bait," he will say. "One boat even got weighted down and sank. Aren't biting now, though."

But I am not discouraged by these words. I stomp to my boat, determined that I will make him eat these words. And I may stuff a soft craw down his throat to boot!

Once I get everything arranged in the bottom of the boat, I grab the oars and start to pull for some point on the oppose shore. I do this automatically because by now I know that the best place to fish is always on the other side of the lake.

After successfully drowning a dozen minnows and two dozen night crawlers, I tend to get discouraged. But then I remember I have a couple of hellgrammites and that a recent article in a fishing magazine said that they are like "candy" for bass. It even shows an eight-year-old boy leaning nonchalantly against a monstrous bass, which he caught naturally with a hellgrammite.

What the article forgot to mention was that every hellgrammite has a couple of pinchers which it does not mind using whenever one insults it by running a cold fishhook up its spine. The hellgrammite is repulsive enough that, once down in the water, it frightens away the boldest of bass.

My live bait has failed, but that kind of fishing was made for country boys anyhow. There is still the artificial bait—including such famous lures as the wounded mouse, the ruptured pike minnow and the compound-fractured frog—all of which are in various stages of orthopedic disrepair. Because of their crippled and rundown conditions, they are supposed to look especially appetizing to fish. However, in reality, they are poor lures because they are larger than most of the fish in the lake.

On one of my better casts, the plug will shoot off in the air at a 60-degree angle and then drop vertically into the water like a hunk of lead. I smack my lips and reel in with great anticipation because undoubtedly the splash has sufficiently angered a fish to take my lure. However, if the cast is a poor one—and a few of them are—the line will tie itself in a knot when the plug has gone out about 20 feet and then, reversing its direction, will land in the boat or else sail by overhead and strike the water somewhere behind me.

Having been blessed with neither the presence of a fish nor the patience of Job, I usually start back to shore after six or seven hours of industrious fishing. I have been beaten again.

The fish have won, but they don't get off so easily! Standing on the dock, I shake my fist violently, promising to return another day with better bait and more patience. This stinging rebuff sends the smallest fish straight to the cold depths of the lake, and it even makes the largest six-inch perch shudder a little.

This ceremony also serves another purpose. Usually it will bring upon the scene a young lad with a willow pole, bent hook and a string of five perch, which he will part with for the price of $2.

With a sigh of satisfaction I heave the fish over my shoulder and start manufacturing my tale about "the *big* one that got away."

Tennis: Love It But Don't Leave It

They say if you pick up a calf every day of its life, you can still lift it after it becomes a full-grown cow. It is with great faith in this witticism that I approach tennis after my 60th birthday. If I play tennis regularly a few times each week, although I may never be able to lift a cow, I should be able to continue the sport the rest of my life. After all, King Gustaf VI of Sweden lived 90 years and played tennis to the end.

But I keep noticing many of my contemporaries emerging from the locker room wearing all sorts of arm and leg supports as they limp onto the courts. They look like the walking wounded. If all of that paraphernalia were laid along I-75, I am convinced it would span Montgomery County from one end to the other. At least there would be enough inventory to start an orthopedic appliance shop.

Tennis, after my 50th birthday, was marked with a degree of frustration. My mind kept sending signals but my body didn't re-spond in a timely manner. I kept telling myself, "You're just 25

"Are you O.K.?" I asked, almost afraid to look.

years too late on that shot." I also found myself walking a little slower as we changed sides and taking a little longer to towel off at the net.

My doctor suggested that I "lob" off a few pounds, but that requires real sacrifice, and furthermore, the only "lob" I was interested in was the kind that soars over my opponent's head and puts some points on the board.

But my spirits were revived recently.

Our usual foursome was playing at the Virginia Hollinger Courts in Oakwood. All my life I had wanted to return the ball with so much "English" on it that it would bounce back to my side of the court without my opponent laying a racquet on it.

On Thursday, June 4, 1987, at 6:19 p.m. I made such a shot, although, I must confess, quite accidentally. My opponent only watched in amazement as the ball eluded him. If he had so much as touched it with his racquet on either side of the net without hitting the net, the point would have been his.

After making the shot, I walked briskly toward the club house.

"Where are you going?" queried Mark.

"To the locker room to shower," I said.

"Why?" asked Jack.

"I intend to sign autographs after I freshen up."

"Get back here and finish this set!" shouted Bill.

My English shot did not impress my fellow players that much. But to me it was like a fisherman catching a once-in-a-lifetime muskie.

Now back to the "walking wounded." I have noticed a direct proportion to the age of the player and the size of his racket. As the player matures, his racket gets larger. So I probably need to consider a bigger racket. Mine has been an embarrassment anyway. One side says "Spaulding" and the other says "Best," as in Best Products. Thus, I seldom offer to spin my racket to see who will serve first, and as I walk about the courts I keep the "Best" side turned toward my body.

The question is: Could an average tennis player—me, for

example—buy a Prince racket with a 50 percent larger control zone, play with Wilson's Rally balls, which are 7 percent larger than regular balls, and thus improve his performance by 57 percent? I intend to find out.

And, oh yes, might I occasionally play with Penn's can of four balls and conserve 25 percent more energy in ball retrieval?

In any event, I intend to keep on swinging. Tennis has been a family activity with a degree of sentiment attached to it, relating back to my parents' first meeting on a tennis court in West Milton in the early 1900s.

We have played for fun, obviously, not fame or fortune.

I remember hitting a terrific overhead slam in the '40s. My younger brother, Dave, took the full impact on his forehead and went down. A minute later he got up, still dazed

"Are you OK?" I asked, almost afraid to look.

"Oh yes," he replied. "I always wear my eyebrows sideways like this."

Good luck to all players over 50. Keep on swinging!

V

I'D RATHER BE RIGHT THAN BE PRESIDENT

Potomac Puzzle
I doubt if George ever threw
That buck across the river blue.
But a dollar then they say,
Went much further than today.

Henry Clay said, "I would rather be right than be president." But today's presidential nominees often get Clay's quote turned around—"I'd rather be president than be right."

Abundant quantities of humor start at the lips of presidents. The sad part is that often they're *not* trying to be funny. Presidential humor is usually collected and published by some editor under a title much like Bill Adler's *The Kennedy Wit.*

In a recent guest column, I toyed with the idea of running for president myself. Since I own a barn, I wanted to form a "Barn Gang" as Charles Kettering did to invent the self starter. I wanted my Barn Gang to be a think tank for conservative ideas and to make a national impact. My idea went over like a porcupine in a balloon factory. Only *one* reader agreed to join the Barn Gang.

In 1988 and 1992, I wrote guest columns suggesting that Erma Bombeck throw her bonnet into the ring, and I sent her some campaign buttons. While she didn't run for president, she did respond humorously each year, writing a column toying with the idea. In 1988, she wrote, in part:

> ...Then I got a letter from an attorney in Ohio saying he was running me for President of the United States. His name is Thomas Cecil, Kettering, Ohio, and he is beating the crabgrass roots on my behalf to "put a little life in the White House."
>
> Tom, believe me when I tell you I am flattered by the offer and the buttons, "BUCKEYES FOR

President John F. Kennedy enjoys a lighter moment with the
White House Press Corps on January 24, 1963.

(Photo courtesy of The Bettmann Archive, New York)

BOMBECK" and "BILL FOR FIRST MAN," but the truth is, I don't want to be President....

    ...I'm bored to death with the responsibility of telling people what to do and when to do it, making new laws and enforcing them and serving as a mediator to promote peace. I don't want to work with Congress. Heaven knows, I've raised enough children....

Four years later in 1992, she wrote, in part:

    This is the second time Tom Cecil, an Ohio attorney, has offered to spearhead my run for the presidency of the United States.

    In 1988, I turned him down because the position is a dead-end job for women. We're looking for something at a higher entry level. Tom is persuasive. There's no getting around that. "We face big problems," he wrote. "After swearing in Bush, we found he was a broccoli basher. Worse yet, he couldn't keep his sushi down. We also found his lips were not properly synchronized when he said 'No new taxes!'"

Politicians or their spouses come up with strange ideas, especially in presidential election years. For example, Hillary Clinton recently reported that she and the president were considering conceiving or adopting a baby. Obviously the idea of producing an election-year baby was *ill conceived*. Even Democrats were chuckling. Or notice Bob Dole's query: "If you parents weren't here, who would you want to raise your children, Bill Clinton or me?" Polls indicated that most parents preferred President Clinton. Probably the question should have been, "Who would be your favorite grandfather?"

    President Calvin Coolidge was sparse with words. He became known as "Silent Cal." After attending church alone one Sunday morning, Cal returned to the White House and was greeted by his wife, Grace. The conversation went like this.

Grace: "How was the sermon?"
Cal: "Fine."
Grace: "What was the sermon about?"
Cal: "Sin."
Grace: "What did the minister say about it?"
Cal: "He was against it."

The president with the best sense of humor was Abraham Lincoln. Humor was part of the formula that helped the war-weary president through the difficult Civil War period. At cabinet meetings Lincoln sometimes read excerpts from a book written by humorist, Artemus Ward.

James C. Humes, in *The Wit and Wisdom of Abraham Lincoln*, relates the following:

> In 1865, a Richmond woman came to Lincoln to complain of the damage to her house. She demanded that the government give her an award of restitution and relief. Lincoln told her it was Virginia that had seceded and initiated the war. He then added, "This reminds me of the man who murdered his parents and then pleaded for mercy on the grounds that he was an orphan."

Lincoln also had some pithy one-liners like "A man's legs should be long enough to reach the ground." But my all time favorite is, "God must have loved the common man because he made so many of them."

Eventually we will elect a woman president. This will be a step forward after electing 41 men. Barbara Bush hinted at this in a commencement address delivered at Wellesley College on June 1, 1990. She said: "Somewhere out in this audience may even be someone who will one day follow in my footsteps, and preside over the White House as the president's spouse. I wish *him* well!"

While it is fun to study the lighter side of the presidency, we must, at the same time, understand that serving as president is a burdensome and sometimes unrewarding job. Harry Truman probably said it best—"The buck stops here!"

54

"Cherrygate" or The Unlawful Harvesting of Cherry Trees in Virginia

Did he or didn't he? I mean George Washington. Did he or didn't he wing a silver dollar across the Potomac? And did he really do a *hatchet job* on the cherry tree?

For certain, George never threw a dollar across the Potomac. (Even though we'd all agree that a dollar went much farther in those days than now). The place in the river where the event supposedly happened is simply too wide—almost a mile. Baseball's best outfielder couldn't throw a dollar that far!

I understand that a little community of Scots is ensconced on the banks of the Potomac still looking for that dollar.

But "Cherrygate," the unlawful harvesting of cherry trees in Virginia, is more plausible. There is strong evidence that George indeed chopped down the famous cherry tree. The story was first told by Mason Locke Weems, rector of the Mount Vernon parish, in a book published about 1800. Additionally, researchers at the Library of Congress have unearthed some interesting evidence. In a book called *Pictures of Early New York on Dark Blue Staffordshire Pottery*, there is information about an earthenware mug from Germany between 1770 and 1790. On the mug is a drawing of a cut-down cherry tree. Beside it is a young man dressed in the fashion of the Continental Period. The letters "G.W.," a large hatchet and the numerals "1776" also appear on the drawing.

I choose to think the story is true. It has a great object lesson for our children. ("I did it with my own little hatchet.") After all, G.W. could have taken the Fifth: "*Axe* me no questions."

Actually, I think the lad was caught red-handed and confessed to his father in order to avoid a strapping. Circumstantial evidence did him in—the axe was still smoking, wood chips were in his cuffs, a bird's egg was in his hair, a cherry stain was on his cheeks and his fingers were nervously strumming the stump.

At an antiques shop in Washington, D.C., in the '50s, I had an opportunity to buy Washington's axe for $100—a tidy sum for a struggling young lawyer. I decided to buy it as an investment, but just as I was handing over the money the clerk said, "Of course, it's had three new heads and six new handles since George used it."

As you eat your piece of cherry pie on Feb. 22, I hope you will ponder not only the legends of this giant amongst our presidents, but also his lasting impact upon our country.

Lincoln probably said it best on Feb. 22, 1842: "His is the mightiest name on earth—long since mightiest in the cause of civil liberty, still mightiest in moral reformation. On that name a eulogy cannot be spoken. To add brightness to the sun or glory to the name of Washington is alike impossible. Let none attempt it. In solemn awe we pronounce the name, and in its naked, deathless splendor leave it shine on . . . Washington."

"Scalpgate" At $200 A Clip

The words "scalpgate" or "hairgate" should not surprise us as the name appended to the most famous and possibly most expensive presidential haircut in history. Surely at $200, the President was *clipped* in more ways than one. The tendency to describe questionable behavior by adding "gate" followed Watergate. Thus "Irangate," dealing with unlawful arms sales; "Rubbergate," describing bounced checks in the House Bank and "Travelgate," involving the recent travel office fiasco in the White House.

While not agreeing with President Clinton's positions, I confess to a hearty dose of envy when it comes to his full head of gray hair with no thinning or bald spots. This started back in the New Hampshire Primary where I noted that Clinton was the *mane* contender.

Clinton's recent hairy experience sent me to the *World Book* to review the hairlines of all our presidents this side of 1900. My

At $200, the President was *clipped* in more ways than one.

conclusion is that Clinton wins in a *hairslide,* with JFK a distant second.

In the 1800s, being born in a log cabin proved to be an asset for presidential aspirants. Now in urban society we must adjust to other criteria:

Father: "Son, would you like to grow up to be president?"

Son: "I dunno. Do they have Nintendo games in the White House?"

Father: "Better than that, they've got a war room with all the latest technology. You could spend 24 hours a day there."

Son: "But how can I become president?"

Father: "Do everything your parents and teachers tell you to do, brush your teeth up and down instead of sideways, help senior citizens across the street and take great care of your hair, washing, shampooing and conditioning it often. Early on place your hair care in the hands of a stylist who is good but not expensive. And best to go for gray hair."

How important is a shock of good hair to success in any business? Sports enthusiast Don King, himself the keeper of an unusual shock of hair, is quoted in a *Sports Illustrated*, December 10, 1990, column entitled "From Hair To Eternity." King says, "You can't become a sports immortal without follicles of fabulous fecundity."

Thus, could a hair-impaired (to be politically correct) candidate be elected to office today? President Eisenhower, with his Daddy Warbucks image and contagious smile, was hair-impaired by today's standards. Could he have made it to the Oval Office in 1992?

Clinton's problem is one of sincerity. With the large gap between campaign promises and presidential performance, one wonders if you pulled his hair, might it come off in your hand. The June 7, 1993, issues of two periodicals discussed the event as follows: "His balmy decision," says *Time* magazine, "to have his hair trimmed on Air Force One by a Beverly Hills coiffure, put the presidential scalp in national headlines." And "The first locks," as *Newsweek* referred to them, "added a fall of Rome air to the White House's (other) troubles."

The Clinton campaign projected a populist candidate who related to the common man. Remember the Clinton who boarded a Greyhound bus after the convention to meet people at the grass roots level? With his $200 haircut, he has taken taxpayers, including me, to the *cutting edge* of tolerance. How can he look any of us in the eye and ask us for "shared sacrifice"? His trimming aboard *Hair* Force One takes its place among other gaffs that have dropped his approval rating to 36 percent.

Not to miss an opportunity, Ross Perot televised his $10 cut that set his prominent ears out even further. Reagan and Bush apparently paid $12 to $15 for haircuts from the White House barber. Former Bush press secretary Marlin Fitzwater observed that the White House, with its numerous problems, should have "a few more fat old bald men." Fitzwater himself fights the "battle of the bald." The former white House barber Milton Pitts observed, "I would have given it (President Clinton's haircut) more of an oval look. If you look at it, the top of his head looks pointed." I wonder if the "oval look" is an unintentional pun trying to make Clinton look presidential and ready for the Oval Office.

My conclusion is that Clinton is not a populist. The $200 haircut financed with the President's own money may seem trivial, but it is symbolic of excessive congressional and presidential spending within the beltway where millions, billions and trillions of taxpayers' money is mainlined into the porkbarrel or wasted. I do not want to pay a dime more in taxes until the Washington mess is cleaned up.

Who—If Anyone—Zapped Zachary?

I'm glad the president received a clean bill of health! I'm not talking about President Bush. Rather, I'm referring to Zachary Taylor, who checked out in 1850.

Clara Rising of Holder, Florida, theorized that Z.T. was assassinated by eating fruit laced with arsenic a few days before he died. If true, Taylor would be our first martyred president, while Lincoln would be our second victim of assassination. Ms. Rising conjectures that Taylor was done in by Southerners angered by Taylor's stance on slavery.

I have some problems with digging up and examining a corpse 141 years old. If foul play were demonstrated, what next? Dig up someone else and try him or her for murder? In any event, the autopsy was conducted in Louisville a few weeks ago; it showed an absence of arsenic in tissue from Taylor's body. I'm glad we don't have to rewrite history.

But while the spotlight is on our twelfth president, here's some trivia you should know:

- Taylor was one of seven presidents born in a log cabin.

- General Taylor distinguished himself as an Indian fighter. He also served in the War of 1812 and the Mexican War. He was the Eisenhower of his day.

- Zachary's wife, Margaret MacKall Smith, smoked a corncob pipe, as did President Jackson's wife. She was somewhat of a recluse who didn't want her husband to be president. She spent much time knitting in her room. Taylor's daughter, Betty Bliss, often filled in as official hostess on her mother's behalf.

- In spite of the corncob pipe, Taylor and his wife had a son and five daughters, one of whom, Sarah, married Jefferson

Davis, the future president of the Confederacy. Sarah died three months after her wedding. The son, Richard, was a Lieutenant General in the Confederate Army.

- Taylor's troops called him "Old Rough and Ready." He patched his clothes and wore them until they couldn't be patched any longer.

- General Taylor wore his uniform on formal occasions only. On the battlefield he wore civilian clothes. One of his soldiers said, "He always wears an old cap, dusty green coat, a frightful pair of trousers, and on horseback he looks like a toad."

- A letter was sent "postage due" from the Whig Convention to Z. T. at Baton Rouge notifying him of his nomination for President. Taylor unwittingly refused to pay the postage and the letter was returned to the senders.

- Taylor never held any elective office before he became president, and he never voted in a presidential election until he voted for himself in 1848.

- Since Inauguration Day fell on a Sunday, Taylor postponed his swearing in from March 4, 1849, to March 5, 1849. Indeed, some historians claim that David Rice Atchison, president pro tem of the Senate, was president for one day. Dying in 1886, his monument modestly claims: "David Rice Atchison, 1807-1886. President of U.S. for one day. Lawyer, statesman and jurist."

- On April 10, 1849—36 days into Taylor's administration— the safety pin was invented by Walter Hunt. (Taylor had nothing to do with this.)

- Taylor was one of ten presidents who were Episcopalians.

- Taylor is our only president whose initials are Z.T.

- Zachary Taylor was a second cousin of James Madison, our fourth president. President Franklin Roosevelt was related by blood or marriage to eleven first families, one of whom was Taylor.

- No one ever wrote a book entitled *The Wit of Zachary Taylor*.

- On July 4, 1850, Taylor attended the laying of the cornerstone of the Washington Monument. Exposed to the hot sun for many hours, he developed a high fever and died five days later.

- Taylor's favorite horse, "Whitey," a war hero, grazed on the White House lawn. When Taylor died after 16 months in office, old Whitey followed his master's body in the funeral procession.

Democrats Make Being a Republican Fun

I like Democrats almost as much as Republicans. In fact, the Democratic Party is my second favorite political organization. I am a strong believer in the two-party system. If it weren't for Democrats, being a Republican wouldn't be any fun.

Democrats deliver our babies and our mail. They repair our cars, teach our children, prepare our tax returns, design our buildings, pilot our planes, write our books, construct our houses, fight our wars, assist little old ladies across the street, help their kids with homework, attend P.T.A meetings and sit next to us in church.

Like me, the average Democrat desires good government. Probably, come to think of it, the average Democrat wants a little *more* government than I want.

But in spite of their many good traits, I wonder if there are too many Democrats. I had this sneaking suspicion that there were more of "them" than "us." My hunch was confirmed when I called Kay Stephens, Director of The Montgomery County Board of Elections for registration information.

In the May Primary in 1988, there were 100,084 Democrats who voted, or 33 percent. The Republicans, however, could claim only 59,306 who voted, or 20 percent. Finally, that great swing group of unaffiliated or independent voters totalled 142,439, or 47 percent.

I checked with my daughter, Rebecca, who majored in sociology at O.S.U., and it was her opinion that the rate of increase in population for Democrats was substantially greater than for Republicans, the Democrats apparently having taken more seriously the biblical command to "Be fruitful and multiply." I reckoned that by the year 2027, my party could be as dead as the "mugwumps," an offshoot of the Republican party that died out in the late 1800s.

With the presidential election less than two months away (November, 1988), the above figures alarmed me. My immediate reaction was that Republicans should be placed on the endangered species list. Legislation with respect to endangered species is set forth in the Conservation Section of the U.S. Code. Congress has found that "various species of fish, wildlife and plants in the U.S. have been rendered extinct." The ensuing legislation encourages all federal agencies to conserve endangered species. When the Department of Interior sends me the application I requested, I shall describe the species by its biological name: *Republicanus*. With such a fancy Latin name, this just might get through.

But should the Republicans throw in the towel—or elephant— so to speak? Both parties have been in despair from time to time. For example, through my grade school and high school years,

Franklin Roosevelt was the popular peace and wartime president. The landscape was strewn with his political victims. I well remember three defeated Republican candidates: Landon (1936), Wilkie (1940), and Dewey (1944 and 1948). Hoover also was defeated by FDR in my lifetime (1932), but I was too young to remember it. During these discouraging years I wondered if the Roosevelt reign would ever end in my lifetime.

Not only has there been a scarcity of peanuts for the elephant from time to time, but also the Democrat donkey has occasionally found slim grazing. From our first post-Civil War president, Democrat Andrew Johnson, to Democrat Woodrow Wilson, spanning almost fifty years, there was only one Democrat elected president. This was Grover Cleveland. Electing a Democrat was such a shock that the voters gave him a split shift. He was elected in 1884, defeated in 1888 and reelected in 1892. If you were a Democrat voter either before or after the Cleveland terms, you probably would have said, "When, oh when, will these Republicans be driven from the White House?"

I was concerned about Cleveland during the term he sat out since unemployment compensation had not yet been invented. But I found that he actually enjoyed himself, practicing law, signing autographs, posing for pictures, kissing babies and reminding his countrymen and countrywomen that things were going to the dogs under Benjamin Harrison, a Republican.

I hope that, confronted with the above registration figures, you Democrats and Independents, as a matter of fairness, will conserve, preserve, encourage and nurture your Republican friends. Between now and November 8, why not take one or more of the following actions:

- If you are a farmer, stable an elephant in your barn. During the day tether it in your pasture with a Bush sign in its trunk.

- Accept campaign material joyfully from your Republican friends. Place that bumper sticker on your car and that button

on your shirt or blouse.
- Turn the TV up louder when Bush commercials are on.

- Baby-sit Republican infants so their parents may go door-to-door with their materials.

- Mail evergreen seedlings to registered voters with "Beat the bushes for Bush" tags on them.

Ohio will be a real battleground in the next several weeks. Both the Dukakis and Bush managers agree that the Buckeye State is a toss-up right now. The candidates with their shrill voices will crisscross our state several times before Election Day. In the course of events, the donkey's ears will be pulled and the elephant's trunk will be tweaked.

But you and I, in spite of the excesses of our favorite candidates, need to remain good friends and be on speaking terms after the election.

After all, we are the backbone of the two-party system!

Trouble on the Line

It's Friday—usually a good day. But at 3:10 p.m. my phone rings.

Me: "Hello."
Suzy: "Mr. Cecil, I'm Suzy from the Republican National Committee."
Me: "Great! It's my favorite political organization."
Suzy: "We're trying to mount a tremendous media campaign to try to neutralize all those misstatements they're telling about Gingrich and Dole."
Me: "Let me come right to the point. I never agree to a

dollar amount over the phone."

Suzy: "I understand. But can we put you down for $200?"

Me: "No."

Suzy: "OK. Maybe..."

Me: "Let me be frank with you. I really like Senator Dole..."

Suzy: "$75?"

Me: "No. In fact I was born into the Republican Party in 1927."

Suzy: "Really! How about $65?"

Me: "No numbers please, Suzy."

Suzy: "OK. But maybe just $55?"

Me: "I'd like for you to deliver some free advice to Senator Dole."

Suzy: "Fine. Maybe ..."

Me: "First, tell the senator he needs to smile more."

Suzy: "Yes, I certainly agree, but..."

Me: "Next, tell him he should stop calling himself 'Bob Dole' in his speeches. He *is* Bob Dole and should use pronouns like 'me' or 'I' when referring to himself."

Suzy: "Good idea, but maybe $45?"

Me: "Nope. Also tell him to get off this who-would-you-rather-your-kids-have-as-a-father kick. A recent poll showed that 52 percent of parents preferred Clinton and that actually he, Dole, comes across with more of a grandfather image, like Eisenhower."

Suzy: "How about $35?"

Me: "No. Furthermore, Dole said he was devising a strategy to 'get' the women's vote. Why be so obvious?"

Suzy: "Maybe $25?"

Me: "No numbers, please, Suzy. Additionally, Senator Dole tells us what his *focus groups* have told him. Why doesn't he keep some things to himself? He shouldn't tell us everything he knows each time he opens his mouth. If he's not careful, he might even lose Oakwood."

Suzy: "That's right. Surely $15 would be OK."

Me: "Negative. Also tell him he needs to give a lot of thought to selecting his VP. He needs to choose a man or woman decidedly younger than he, and from a Midwestern state like Ohio, which almost always goes for the winner. For example, Rep. John Kaisch would do nicely."

Suzy: "OK with me, but..."

Me: Put me down for $100, Suzy, and I'll send my check. I was purposely arguing with you to help you persevere when talking to grumpy old men. If we all work hard together, we can change things in Washington!

To Run or Not to Run—That Is the Question

Alright, alright, ALRIGHT already. I may do it, but I just don't want to be rushed. After all, I have until the end of December to make up my mind.

Faced with the same decision, Civil War General William T. Sherman said, "I do not seek the office. If nominated, I won't run and if elected, I won't serve." For my own part, I'm just not ready to make a "Shermanesque" statement with respect to 1996. However, I admit that I requested papers from the Federal Election Commission in Washington, D.C. and that on my desk are forms FEC 1 (Statement of Organization) and FEC 2 (Statement of Candidacy), together with several instruction booklets explaining how I, my committee and treasurer can stay out of jail.

But I just don't know what to say about running. Essentially,

I hesitate humbly, since I know the office must seek the man.
But I will never shirk, if duty calls.

I'm waiting to hear from my people.

Actually, my candidacy shrinks by comparison to other occupants of the Oval Office. I don't have a full shock of hair like Kennedy or pet beagles named "Him" and "Her" like LBJ. I can't speak "Nixonese" ("I want to make this *perfectly clear"*) or stumble off airplanes like Jerry Ford. Further, I don't have a Pepsodent smile or peanut farm like Jimmy Carter. I was not blessed with Reagan's charisma and never have I been clipped for a $200 haircut on Air Force One per Clinton.

In the old days, the question was posed, "Is he (the candidate) presidential timber?" I'm not sure how that applies to me. One of my people was talking about a "Draft Cecil" movement. I told him I thought I had done enough in 1945 as Mailman 3rd Class on the U.S.S. Kenneth Whiting and didn't want to go into the service again. More confusing was a suggestion that I be a "dark horse."

I just don't know what to do. I hesitate humbly, since I know the office must seek the man. But I will never shirk, if duty calls.

It is true that I have fleshed out a cabinet in the event I am inaugurated January 20, 1997. I can't release these names now. However, I can tell you that my cabinet will be diverse, reflecting the face of my Christmas card list—if not the face of the nation. I want to name people I can work with. None of these people have an embarrassing "nannygate" problem lurking in their closets. This much I can tell you. One-half of my cabinet will wear bow ties.

In the 1988 primaries, I suggested that Erma Bombeck toss her bonnet into the ring. In turning down the offer she wrote in her column, "I don't want to work with Congress. Heaven knows, I've raised enough children." In this same sense, I feel overqualified to work with a difficult Congress.

Although not born in a log cabin, I am fortunate to have a two-story barn behind my house. I want to form a "Barn Gang" as Kettering did when the self-starter was invented. The gang will meet periodically in my barn and act as conservative advisers in the event I am forced into a campaign.

The Barn Gang will not try to "reinvent government" since

Clinton and Gore have already tried this and failed. What they don't know is that government was successfully invented 208 years ago. We need to reinvent the integrity of those who run our government. And, frankly, before Gore does anything more, he needs to take a course on how to keep his audiences from yawning off on him as he speaks.

So please be patient with me. Give me time to test the waters and make the most important decision in my life. In the meantime, I have no problem with your circulating "Cecil" buttons or asking for an application to be part of the "Barn Gang."

VI

TAXATION *WITH* REPRESENTATION— OUR WORST NIGHTMARE

Representation (Or Can We Afford It?)
"No taxation without representation,"
Our ancestors said without hesitation.
But now with congressmen and senators too
There's hardly enough left over for you!

"A great civilization is not conquered from without until it has destroyed itself within. The essential causes of Rome's decline lay in her people, her morals, her class struggle, her failing trade, her bureaucratic disposition, her *stifling taxes*, her consuming wars." (Emphasis added.) These words were written by Will Durant, an American historian, philosopher and educator, in 1944. Apparently the Romans were overtaxed 2,000 years ago.

In describing a person's career, we sometimes say, "He got mixed up in politics." Politics has been defined as the art and science of the government of a state. (By implication, the federal government too.) Thus, our politics as such are not mixed up but there are a number of *mixed up politicians*.

Simply stated, as U.S. citizens and voters, our taxes are driven by pork, perks, waste, fraud, deficit spending, logrolling and boondoggles. We are frustrated as we see politicians obsessed compulsively with the expenditure of *our* money. President Bush warned us in 1992 to be wary of any politician who is going to *give* you something. His advice: "Hang on to your wallet."

Our government has become too big, too costly and too intrusive. In many instances, we are ruled by mindless, faceless bureaucrats who thrive and seem to multiply like coat hangers in your closet. We have too much bureaucracy. To get to someone who is accountable, one needs to peel back several layers of bureaucrats, much as we peel layers off an onion.

71

One of the following columns deals with Tax Freedom Day. Most taxpayers are not aware that they work from January 1 to early May of each year to finance several layers of government. What would happen if income taxes were not deducted from our paychecks and tax money would be sent to Washington, Columbus and Dayton by individual taxpayers? Suddenly, taxpayers would become aware of the terrific drain taxes make on family incomes. It is to be hoped that knowledgeable taxpayers would become energized and make known their complaints to politicians.

One of the problems is the IRS. Although they work for us, they are not user-friendly. The tax code, consisting of several thousand pages and millions of words, needs to be simplified since even the IRS doesn't understand all of it. Simplifying the tax code would result in downsizing the number of IRS employees. The *Reader's Digest* has done an admirable job of exposing IRS excesses. A May 1993 article, entitled "The Mess at the IRS," is worth reading. The present tax code should be scrapped in total. Legislators should go back to the drawing board and fashion laws that are understandable and workable. One benefit of the presidential primaries in 1996 has been to focus our attention on alternate tax plans.

For many years I complained and wrote about excessive taxation and other problems. Finally, in 1993 I took decisive action. I started a newsletter called *Porkbusters II*. The original Porkbusters are congressmen of both parties in Washington devoted to exposing and eliminating pork and waste from our federal budgets.

The purpose of my newsletter is to encourage citizen action at a grass roots level. My subscribers, scattered across 50 states, are urged to write letters to the editor, call talk shows, contact congressmen, encourage qualified candidates to run for office and support them with contributions, volunteer work, votes and prayers.

Porkbusters II is mailed four times per year and is free to subscribers. My cost is less than a dollar a day, and I would rather finance this than pay taxes.

My fervent hope is that *you* will get involved in the tax process. You can make a difference!

Our Fathers Brought Forth upon This Nation a New Tax (1953)

I notice a memorial is to be erected to Franklin D. Roosevelt in Washington, D.C. It would be "altogether fitting and proper" that the Taxpayers' Gettysburg Address be inscribed on one of the walls of the memorial. I received it on a postcard in 1953. The author's name was not shown. Here it is, with apologies to A. Lincoln:

One score and eighteen years ago our fathers brought forth upon this nation a new tax, conceived in desperation and dedicated to the proposition that all men are fair game.

Now we are engaged in a great mass of computations testing whether that tax or any taxpayer so confused can long endure. We are met on Form 1040, the battlefield of that tax. We have come to dedicate a large part of our income to a final resting place in the hands of those men who spend their lives so that they may spend our money.

It is altogether unfitting and improper that they should do this. But in the legal sense we cannot evade, we cannot avoid, we cannot underestimate this tax. Our congressmen, living and dead, have determined it beyond our power to add or subtract.

Our creditors will little note nor long remember what we pay here, but the Bureau of Internal Revenue can never forget what we report here. It is rather for us to be dedicated to the great task remaining before us, that from these vanishing dollars we take increased devotion to the few remaining; and that we here highly resolve that taxes of the people, by the people and from the people shall some day perish from the earth.

Will Rogers and His Joke Factory on Handicap Hill (1990)

"Every time they (Congress) make a joke," quipped Will Rogers, "it's a law. And every time they make a law, it's a joke."

Rogers' humorous newspaper columns entertained millions of Americans from 1922-1935. "Will considered Congress his private hunting preserve," wrote his biographers, Bryan and Frances Sterling. "It was his 'Joke Factory' located on Handicap Hill."

He once wrote, "l just got back from Washington, D.C. (Department of Comedy). I had heard that the Congressional Show was to close on June 7th."

Will Rogers would have a heyday if he were writing today.

What do studies dealing with flatulence in cows and the effects of low flying jet planes on pregnant horses have in common? Give up? Both of them were financed by appropriations from the federal government. You, the taxpayer, footed the bill!

Earlier this year, the study on pregnant horses involved $100,000 of your funds.

Flatulence in cows was explained by columnist Mike Royko. The Senate was studying the farm bill when Senator Symms pointed out that part of the bill provided for spending $19 million to study methane emissions from cattle as it relates to global warming and the greenhouse question. He claimed that he was not ready to face his constituents and tell them they must be taxed for this project. (Probably Senator Symms was thinking that there is no substantial problem with cows emitting methane gas, unless, of course, *you* are standing next to one.)

But, after raising the issue, the Senator threw in the towel in this fashion:

"I appeal to my colleagues... and I do not want to force them to some embarrassing vote, but I think it pretty hard to explain to the voters of the United States who feel they are already overtaxed."

As taxpayers we would ask, Why not force a vote on such a bill? This bovine departure from sanity in Rogers' "Department of Comedy" drives us to *udder* distraction. Obviously, the taxpayer is being *milked*.

What we need is a David to rise up from the Senate floor and slay the Goliath of shameless government waste. Such a Senator would not be popular among his colleagues but would be a folk hero on Main Street, U.S.A., ending up not only on network TV news, but also the Carson, Letterman and Donahue shows.

I am not so naive as to believe that elimination of the two boon-doggles mentioned above could make a sizable dent in our deficit. However, a principle is involved. At a time when we are being asked to tighten our belts and pay more taxes, Congress is not willing to eliminate "fluff" in the budget nor seriously attack the pork barrel.

We need another Senator like Everett Dirkson from Illinois, who remonstrated: "A billion here, a billion there and pretty soon you're talking about real money."

Likewise, the 64 cents a year from my taxes that goes to the National Endowment of the Arts will not alone break me. But again a principle is involved. (We will give you culture whether you want it or not!)

The questionable half dozen pictures in the Mapplethorpe collection wisely were not published in local newspapers. The recent Cincinnati jury verdict pushed so-called First Amendment Rights beyond the wildest imaginations of those who authored our Bill of Rights. But more important than obscenity, funding NEA with tax dollars raises a valid issue as to whether the Arts and many other

"A billion here, a billion there and pretty soon
you're talking about real money."

projects should be funded with public or private funds. Abraham Lincoln answered this question around 1854: "The legitimate object of government is to do for the people what needs to be done, but which they cannot, by individual effort, do at all, or do so well for themselves." Honest Abe also reminded us that the government can give us back only that which it first takes away.

Why should federal grants be handed out to artists and performers any more than to carpenters, barbers, lawyers, doctors, architects and others who struggle to set up a new business?

Two recent news articles vividly contrast the issue of public versus private funding. The first article described a $500,000 federal appropriation to renovate the former home of retired bandleader Lawrence Welk and to build tourist accommodations. This was part of—this is true—an agriculture appropriations bill. The second article said that relatives and fans of the late Walt Kelly, creator of *Pogo*, have paid for and dedicated a memorial to the artist at the Okefenokee Swamp in Georgia. As a taxpayer, which project makes the most sense?

The problem of waste is enhanced by the fact that, generally, we send *politicians* to Washington rather than *businessmen or businesswomen*. Accountability is lacking. Your representatives should be like a board of directors of a large corporation that needs to explain to the shareholders its stewardship of their funds.

What can be done to eliminate waste? In one sense, the answer seems obvious. To the compulsive eater we say, "Eat less;" to the alcoholic we say, "Stop drinking" and to the compulsive government spender we need to say, "Spend drastically less." But the problem is complex. It involves a tradition of red-ink spending, logrolling (You vote for my project, and I'll vote for yours), and pressure from well-financed PACS.

But waste and overspending will not stop until taxpayers across the country say stop. Someone has suggested that we should send tea bags to our representatives and senators. If this were taken seriously, one should immediately buy stock in Lipton Tea since millions of citizens are frustrated to the point of despair. As the

Boston Tea Party in 1773 became a symbol of taxpayer revolt, so in 1990 we need a Potomac Tea Party.

Voters from 50 states in boats, rafts, canoes and inner tubes should assemble in Boston Harbor at the actual site of the Boston Tea Party. The armada should sail down the Atlantic coast and up the Potomac River, tying up at the Tidal Basin. Here sailor-taxpayers might deliver petitions with millions of signatures from grass-roots voters to Congress and the President.

Most of all, we need another political-humorist like Will Rogers, who might go to Washington and say, "C'mon folks, get serious!"

Tax Freedom Day—You Made It (1981)

Congratulations! You made it!

Today, May 11, is your tax-free day. The average taxpayer has just worked from January 1 to May 11 to finance, through direct and indirect taxation, four layers of government: federal, state, county and city. In this sense we are all part-time government workers.

Someone observed, "Another man who doesn't have to pass a Civil Service examination to work for the government is the taxpayer."

If you earn more than the average taxpayer, your tax-free day will come later—perhaps on Memorial Day, the Fourth of July or even Labor Day. But if you're average, having worked 132 days to pay your taxes, you may now relax and work the other 233 days to provide necessities for you and your family. Your only concern is double-digit inflation.

One of the slogans of the War of Independence was: '"No Taxation Without Representation!" Can you imagine the astonishment of our ancestors if they should realize that, although we are still free of the British Crown, we have voluntarily burdened ourselves with taxes that we labor 132 days to pay. And this *with* representation!

Yes, taxation without representation is tyranny, but it was a lot cheaper.

The abuse of the power to tax U.S. citizens did not occur to those who wrote our constitution. Although one of the purposes in the Preamble is to "promote the general welfare," it never was intended that through the power of taxation the income of our taxpayers should be *redistributed* among our citizens with every conceivable type of federal welfare program.

What does the fiscal conservative stand for? Abraham Lincoln stated it well, when in 1843, he said: "An individual who undertakes to live by borrowing soon finds his original means devoured by interest, and, next, no one left to borrow from—so must it be with a government."

The liberal, on the other hand, is committed to a different set of maxims: "Tax, tax, tax, spend, spend, spend, elect, elect, elect." These words have sometimes been credited to Franklin Roosevelt. Although there is no evidence that he uttered them, many believe they adequately describe the deficit government spending that started in 1933 and has continued to the present.

The policy of the liberals never was on solid financial ground. The point was forcefully brought home November 4 as taxpayers, already burdened with inflation, rebelled.

Never has the case of conservatism been more eloquently stated than by President Reagan in his Inaugural Address. How appropriate to hear him remind us that "government is not the solution to our problems; government is the problem."

No one will deny that reasonable taxes are necessary to provide basic services, to provide for our common defense, and to furnish the basic living requirements to those citizens who are unable to work. But at what point does the taxpayer have the right to complain?

Since there are liberals and conservatives in both major

Death and taxes may be inevitable,
but being taxed to death is not.

political parties, we should probably drop the labels "Republican" and "Democrat" and regroup under "Conservative" and "Liberal" banners.

For example, Senator William Proxmire, D-Wisconsin, has been the consumer taxpayers' friend. Since 1975, Proxmire has made a monthly "Golden Fleece Award" for the biggest, most ridiculous or most ironic example of government spending or waste.

The first award went to the National Science Foundation for an $84,000 study to determine why people fall in love.

Here are some of the other Golden Fleece Awards: $102,000 went to the National Institute of Alcohol Abuse for a study to find out if drunk fish are more aggressive than sober fish; $27,000 went to the Law Enforcement Assistance Administration for a study to determine why inmates want to escape from prison; $57,800 was wasted by the Federal Aviation Administration for a study of 78 body measurements of airline stewardess trainees, ostensibly to design safety equipment. The study was found to be virtually useless by 55 North American airlines; $2,500 went to determine why people are rude, ill-mannered, cheat and lie on the tennis courts; $46,000 was wasted by the Department of Agriculture for a study to determine how long it takes to fry eggs in a skillet.

Locally we need to look only to Second Street, between Wilkinson and Perry, for an example of ludicrous federal spending. Have you noticed the blue sign across the front of the new federal building? Notice the wiggly red, neon figures on it that look like shorthand or perhaps Arabic. Taxpayers paid $23,000 for the design, manufacture and installation of this sign!

Unfortunately, in addition to wasting thousands of dollars, the government is capable of wasting millions, and even billions, and the less the government cuts down on its spending, the more it makes us cut down on ours. The question: What can be done about it?

Howard Jarvis has given us a sensible answer and a reason for hope. "Death and taxes," said the author of California's Proposition 13, "may be inevitable, but being taxed to death is not."

Thus, the best solution to government waste and excessive taxation is the ballot box. Just as those who spend your money recklessly are elected at the ballot box, so they may also be defeated at the ballot box. Ex-Senators McGovern, Magnuson, Bayh and Church can testify to this!

In addition to the ballot box strategy, the voters should remember the power of the pen. You should by all means write to senators and representatives who vote to appropriate money and encourage them to trim budgets of wasteful and unnecessary projects.

As Mark Twain asked, "What is the difference between a taxidermist and a tax collector?" Give up? "The taxidermist takes only your skin." Happy May 11.

Taxes: Try Paying With A Smile (1993)

Taxes! A laughing matter or an insidious cancer growing on society for several decades? Probably both.

Last month you settled up with Uncle Sam. Some of you filed early and "received" your refund; others joined that long caravan of cars moving in both directions in front of the Post Office and grimaced as postal employees relieved you of your "contribution" at 11:59 p.m.

My purpose is to try to keep you happy in this whole process. Let's tune in to a dialogue between two taxpayers:

First taxpayer: You should pay your taxes with a smile.
Second taxpayer: I tried that but they insisted on cash.

My effort to find humor in the IRS, separating taxpayers from their money started at the public library. I merged the words "taxes" and "humor" in a computer system known as InfoTrak. Expecting a couple of dozen sidesplitting funny citations, I was amazed when InfoTrak advised, "No exact match for: TAXES HUMOR." Apparently InfoTrak thinks taxation is a deadly serious business.

Next I turned to Ben Franklin's famous words. The witty Franklin said, "...in this world nothing can be said to be certain, except death and taxes." Someone revised Franklin's words by observing that at least death doesn't get any worse.

And Howard Jarvis, promoter of California's Proposition Thirteen, noted we shouldn't be "taxed to death." Not to be outdone, Margaret Mitchell, author of *Gone With The Wind*, quipped, "Death and taxes and childbirth! There's never any convenient time for any of them."

Mark Twain wrote in 1910, "Now that word—taxes, taxes, taxes—that is a very sore subject to me. I was so relieved when Judge Leventritt did find something that was not taxable when he said that the commissioner could not tax your patience." Conversely, however, the myriad of forms imposed on us by the IRS can definitely "tax" our brains.

Having established the certainty of taxes, the next question is: How much? A Frenchman, Jean Baptiste Colbert, described taxation as the process of "plucking the goose (so) as to obtain the largest amount of feathers with the least possible amount of hissing."

Taxpayers are on the endangered species list and need protection. Each of us has the government on our payroll. Don't let anyone suggest you are not paying your fair share or should share in the sacrifice until things are made right in Washington.

You may chuckle if you read parts of the 1040 instructions. On page 4, precise estimates are made for dealing with your 1040 as follows: "recordkeeping: 3 hr., 8 min.; learning about the law or the form: 2 hr., 42 min.; preparing the form: 3 hr., 37 min; signing, assembling and sending the form to the IRS: 49 min." Stop, stop, stop, IRS! You're telling me more than I want to know! And what was the cost of hardware, software, supplies, space and man/woman power to collect the data?

More laughter may ensue by turning to page 33, which explains how to make a "gift to reduce the public debt." These instructions apparently are meant for taxpayers who feel they are

Clinton's Simplified 1040 Form

Department of the Treasury—Internal Revenue Service

1040 U.S. Individual Income Tax **1993** Return

Your Social Security Number

Part 1. Income

1. How much money did you make last year?. ▶

2. Send it in. . . . . ▶

3. If you have any questions or comments, please write them in the box provided. . . . ▶

not taxed enough or have a little cash left over after April 15th and want to share it with the government.

Clinton's simplified 1040 Form is on the previous page. The author of this piece is unknown. Since the IRS is *not* user-friendly, no doubt the creator of this form wishes to remain anonymous. The form has had wide circulation across our country by way of fax and copy machines. Reading it may alleviate some of your frustrations.

"Rubbergate" or Congress Attempts to Run a Bank (1991)

The attempt of the House of Representatives to run a private bank for its members was a dismal failure. Rather than fix the bank, the members decided to close it. It is, of course, jolly-good sport to see the excesses of congressmen come under public scrutiny, forcing them into an investigation in which the spotlight of public opinion is finally on them.

But in our willingness to condemn "Rubbergate," let's not lose sight of the big problem. Congressmen have intentionally been writing bad checks on behalf of U.S. citizens for decades!

The planned budget deficit for 1991 is $318 billion. Our national debt is almost $3-1/2 trillion. Your elected officials are spending your money like the proverbial drunken sailor or the ranch hand on payday.

As an investor, you would never buy stock in United States Inc. For many years, the U.S. has been a candidate for a Chapter 11 bankruptcy, and if our congressmen were managers of a private corporation, they would be fired at the first annual meeting.

Boondoggles and pork barrel projects are commonplace on Capitol Hill, as our elected officials spend not only our money, but also that of our unborn grandchildren and great-grandchildren. Unless reform occurs, our country will crash before the year 2000.

World's Largest Corporation is Bankrupt (1995)

The largest corporation in the world is U.S.A. Inc. Consider these facts:
- It has been in continuous existence since Sept. 17, 1787.
- It has 248,709,873 shareholders known as citizens.
- It has a board of directors of 535, 100 of whom are known as senators and 435 of whom are known as representatives.
- Its chief executive officer, known as the president, is the most powerful individual in the world.

Even though this is the world's largest corporation, and even though it may tax its shareholders, the corporation is bankrupt. One of the ways to qualify for bankruptcy is to be unable to pay debts as they mature. When debts come due that the corporation can't pay, it merely borrows more money—a rob-Peter-to-pay-Paul scheme .

Not only is U.S.A. Inc. bankrupt financially; it also is bankrupt of ideas. The board of directors seems to have a spending problem. For 40 years it has spent money we don't have for things we don't need and can't afford. It speaks in terms of "giving" money to shareholders. But the corporation can only give money after it first takes it away.

The CEO speaks a strange language known as doublespeak or governmentese. Thus the corporation does not *spend* money but *invests* it; shareholders are not *taxed* but *make contributions*.

To understand the problem, look at the profit and loss statements of U.S.A. Inc. for the past few years. The budget for fiscal 1995 shows income of $1,342,200,000,000 and expenses of $1,518,300,000,000. Thus the budget is written in red ink to the extent of $176,100,000,000. We spend $5,584 more *per second* than we take in.

The actions of the directors and CEO are unfair to the children and grandchildren of the shareholders, who will pay taxes for the rest of their lives to pay for excesses of the directors and CEO.

Solution: Pay salaries to the board of directors and CEO only for those years in which they pass a balanced budget.

A Lesson From Rip Van Winkle (1995)

Rip Van Winkle was a fictional character created by Washington Irving in *The Sketch Book*. He is described in the *World Book* as a "cheerful ne'er-do-well who (preferred) hunting and fishing to farming and his wife's nagging." Meeting some strange people on one of his hikes, he drank some of their ale and promptly fell asleep. He awakened 20 years later. This must be the longest nap on record.

The important point is not only did Rip sleep 20 years; he also slept through a revolution. Before his nap, British Redcoats were marching in the streets and allegiance was paid to the British colors. Upon awakening, he found that the American Revolution had occurred. British troops were gone and the Stars and Stripes waved over a new country.

Rip was not aware of Nathaniel Hale's "I regret that I have but one life to give for my country." Nor did he know of Whittier's Barbara Fritchie—"Shoot if you must, this old gray head, but spare your country's flag," she said.

He snoozed as Benjamin Franklin proclaimed, "Let us all hang together or most assuredly we shall all hang separately" and as Patrick Henry said, "Give me liberty or give me death."

As he slept, he missed the skirmishes at Lexington and Concord, immortalized by Ralph Waldo Emerson's words: "By the rude bridge that arched the flood, their flag to April's breeze unfurled, here once the embattled farmers stood and fired the shot heard 'round the world." As he caught zzz's, he was unaware of the proclamation of the Declaration of Independence, Paul Revere's midnight ride or the surrender of Cornwallis at Yorktown.

The point is obvious. Might we *sleep* on rights for which our ancestors shed their blood? It is possible that our rights are being slowly eroded by faceless bureaucrats, by executive orders, by thousands of regulations, by legislative action or inaction and by judicial activism?

"Eternal vigilance is the price of liberty," claimed Thomas Jefferson.

In the near future, I will make a pilgrimage to the "rude bridge" where the revolution started. I will visit the old North Church and other shrines of our revolution. I will come back a better person with a greater appreciation of sacrifices made for me more than 200 years ago.

VII

ANIMALS, PETS AND OTHER IRRITATIONS

CAT(astrophe)
We brought the kitty home to stay;
Our hearts were all atwitter;
We loved her every single day;
Until she had a litter.

"Hey, Mom, I found this real cute baby dinosaur over in the next canyon. It looked like he'd been abandoned. Can I bring him back to our cave? I'll take good care of him. Please, **pa-leeze**..."

Several millennia pass....

"Daddy, the kitty's so cute. Can we bring her home? Please, **pa-leeze**. I'll take good care of her."

Relationships between parents, children and pets often start with a question so simple. The puppy is wagging its tail and nuzzling your leg with her nose. The salesperson is strumming his fingers on the counter and you might as well reach for your wallet. You have already lost the battle.

My study reveals that kids have this chromosome that relates to pets. Let's call it the "P" chromosome. It is in our youngsters when they are born but manifests itself more when children learn to walk, talk and beg. It sticks with them until they develop an interest in the opposite sex. Now that you understand the "P" chromosome, it will make life easier for you and your children. I recommend caving in, unless of course a kid tries to spring a baby hippopotamus on you.

Numerous pets have boarded at our house—a dog, seven cats, a parakeet, rabbits, mice, a snake, chameleons (you get them at the circus), turtles, fish, toads, groundhogs (never domesticated) and a goat named Alex.

The promises you elicit from your kids on the way home from the pet shop prove meaningless. The explicit understanding you reach with respect to the kids keeping food and water on hand and cleaning the cage frequently melt into oblivion as your kids find more interesting ways to occupy their time. It turns out that the fine print in your invisible parent/child contract states that you (I mean YOU), the suffering parent, must take over the job of nurturing the menagerie the kids have accumulated.

One of my kids was a nanny to nine cats. She was addicted to them. In three full notebooks she collected pictures, family comments and poems she wrote in tribute to the felines. Later my daughter became an adolescent and cats took second place in her life.

The Fish That Came In From the Cold

News Item: "Fish Helps Nab Poacher"—London wildlife experts studying the migrating habits of a salmon equipped with an electronic tagging device were surprised when the eight-pounder scaled a river bank and raced across the north Wales countryside. It landed on a poacher's kitchen table, and was still there with three other salmon when police arrived to arrest Paul Williams.

Did you ever notice that humorous events often occur in England? After chuckling over the above story, I pictured this scenario:

Chief Higgins: (picking up the telephone) "'Iggins heah of Scotland Yard. 'Ow may I 'elp you?"

Quackenbush: "I'm officer Quackenbush with 'er Majesty's Wildlife Department. I say, a mighty strange thing 'appened in Wales, Sir. Let me tell you...."

Higgins: "Blimey! Unthinkable! You mean you placed a bug in a salmon and it's now journeying by land across north Wales?"

Quackenbush: "Quite right, Sir."

Higgins: "I'll put two of my best chaps on it—Jones-Smith and Smith-Jones."

Quackenbush: "Are you having me on?"

Higgins: "No, of course not. 'Aven't you ever heard of 'yphenated names? These lads are first cousins, you know. Oh! By the way, get your radar tracking equipment here right on."

Jones-Smith: (driving a government-issued Land Rover and turning to Smith-Jones) "I say, ol' chap, this is the first salmon job for me. 'Ow 'bout you?"

Smith-Jones: "Same 'ere. If the case 'adn't come through official channels, I'd say something was fishy in Wales."

Jones-Smith "Clever, Smith-Jones. But remember, we must uphold that old tradition. You know, Scotland Yard always nabs its man—er fish, that is. I'd 'ate to let 'Iggins down."

Smith-Jones: "Clever, old chap. This will be tough. A quid says we'll never see 'ide nor 'air of the bugger."

Jones-Smith: "Maybe you should say we won't see fin nor gill of the bloomin' thing."

(A half hour passes as Jones-Smith and Smith-Jones speed on through country lanes and fields in north Wales, determined to get their fish.)

Smith-Jones: "We must be about a kilometer from the scene of the crime. The dial on this radar is jumping around like a mad 'atter."

Jones-Smith: (Slowing and pulling to a stop on the left side of the road): "I should judge our criminal is in yonder cottage. The one with the 'Williams' sign on the gate."

(The fearless twosome crouch low, seek cover behind bushes, and make their way to the back door of the Williams' cottage.)

Smith-Jones: "O.K. We'll go on three."

(Both men raise one of their legs to shoulder height and simultaneously kick the door mightily on the three count. The unlocked door gives in without resistance, sending a dog and cat yowling to another part of the house. Stunned, an elderly couple sit at a small table across the room. Steam is rising from a platter of salmon. The old man has a fork full of salmon halfway to his mouth.)

Jones-Smith: "Drop that salmon. And if you eat our bug, we'll cut it out of ya right now."

Smith-Jones: "Right! I didn't become 'Er Majesty's servant to preside over the dissolution of 'er salmon industry." (He slips handcuffs on the astonished couple while Jones-Smith empties the salmon into an evidence bag. Drawing himself to his full height, he demands that the couple follow him.)

Jones-Smith: "We got our fish and crooks. Looks like you owe me a quid, mate."

Ostrich Investment Made with Head in the Sand?

Surely the ostrich was designed by a committee—say the Bird Subcommittee of the Agriculture Department. But then again, since its stubby wings don't permit it to fly, it may have been designed by the same guy in the Pentagon who brought us the $700 toilet and the $100 screwdriver. Committees are famous for turning the simple into the complex.

The scientific classification for the ostrich is *Struthionidae Struthio Camelus*. But unless you speak Latin fluently, like the Pope, you should just call it an ostrich.

I never had a close personal relationship with an ostrich. In fact, at the zoo I usually strode past that part of the menagerie at a fast clip, looking straight ahead. Frankly, I felt the bird had been hit with the "ugly stick." Indeed the Bible says the ostrich is an "abomination." (Leviticus 11:16) Therefore, I felt stupid as I recently held the phone to my ear. On the other end of the line some 2,300 miles away on the West coast was the Ostrich Man (hereafter O.M.). He unloaded his slick presentation on me, trying to put some distance between me and $6,250. I could own a part of The Blue Ridge Ostrich Ranch in Texas.

The pitch seemed almost too good to be true. Within two years I could have all of my capital returned. Good "breeders" might escalate in value from $6,000 in three months to $55,000 in 36 months. I learned that ostriches don't bury their heads in the sand although investors—like me for example—might bury their heads in the sand. Against this flowery investment talk, I read in the subscription application to be signed by me, that I "recognized that I might lose all or part of my investment."

Would this be a "high flyer" venture for me? Could I make a dime? I might feather my nest if all goes well and ostrich burgers become the "in" thing. According to the O.M., ostriches multiply like rabbits, but still the demand outruns the supply.

Cared for by a veterinarian, ostriches are generally healthy. They have their own health care plan insuring them against minor problems such as death, disease and infertility. "Breeders" who fail to produce usually end up as steaks, briefcases and feather dusters.

"Cousins are not permitted to mate," the O.M. assured me. I breathed a sigh of relief, but at the same time wondered how these young birds with all those raging hormones were encouraged toward abstinence so as to be paired with an eugenically correct mate. It had something to do with making a small slit in the chick's neck and inserting a computer chip. (I didn't understand.)

The O.M. went on to state that ostriches are monogamous. However, my research in the *World Book* and dictionary showed them to be polygamous. Actually, I really don't care what consenting ostriches do in their spare time, but I wanted the O.M. to know I was knowledgeable and that it would not be easy to pry

To buy or not to buy? Would my family probate me
for even thinking of it?

$6,250 from my checking account.

The video sent by the O.M. was a piece of art, drawing the viewer into the actual operation of the ostrich ranch in Texas. Central in the sales pitch was a young lady—Teresa, the manager. A long-legged, long-haired, blue-jeaned Western beauty, she appeared equally at home on the ranch, nuzzling an ostrich, or with her hair upswept in the board room, studying a computer printout with her staff. She looked as if she had just popped out of *Glamour* magazine. I noticed that no feathers stuck to her and her shiny ostrich boots attested to the fact that she walked carefully in the ostrich patch. After all, ostrich boots retail for between $800 and $2,500 a pair.

Ostrich meat is delicious, according to the O.M., who claimed it was as tasty as steak and more healthy, containing substantially smaller amounts of calories and cholesterol than equal portions of chicken, turkey, beef, lamb and pork. However, nothing he said convinced me to tear up my Pine Club charge card.

But I had a big decision to make. To buy or not to buy? Would my family probate me for even thinking of it? Might bankruptcy be lurking around the corner? Might my ostrich venture turn into a *turkey*? Might...

I slipped my check for $6,250 into the mailbox, realizing that in the end I might end up with egg on my face and the *yolk* on me. Penniless, I might seek out the O.M. on the west coast and ask for a peanut butter—er make that ostrich—sandwich.

A Rabbit out of the Presidential Hat?

With many unsolved problems in the Carter administration, it is reassuring to know that our president successfully defended himself from a rabbit attack while fishing near Plains, Georgia, last spring. (*Journal Herald*, August 30, 1979)

The rambunctious rabbit is reported to have swum (that's right!) toward the Carter canoe, "hissing menacingly, its teeth flashing and nostrils flaring." Bravely, JC beat it back with a canoe paddle. Lest anyone think that Jimmy pulled this rabbit from his hat, a White House photographer took a picture of it and then had it blown up (the picture, not the rabbit). A White House staffer claimed, "It was a killer rabbit, all right."

Perhaps Carter's springtime encounter will give new insight into the expression "wild as a March hare."

The fact that the rabbit was reported to be swimming sent me straight to the *World Book*. Fifteen minutes and three pages later I had learned more about cottontails than I really wanted to know, such as "when chased by an enemy, a rabbit can hop as fast as 18 miles an hour." However, nothing in the *World Book* revealed that a rabbit can swim. "A rabbit moves about," confides the *World Book*," by hopping on its hind legs, which (now brace yourself) are much longer and stronger than its front legs." I also checked with my daughter, Amy, a college senior majoring in biology. She said simply, "Rabbits are not aquatic."

Meanwhile, back at the presidential canoe, we can only wonder what actually happened. Was this a rabid rabbit? An apparition? Swamp gas? A mechanical rabbit freed from the boring spiral of the racetrack? Or, perhaps a tin bunny placed in the water by Teddy Kennedy ready to "watergate" the president with a miniature camera and microphone?

The political implications of putting a canoe paddle to a rabbit can be devastating. What of the votes to be lost by three generations of Uncle Wiggly players? And what of the ballot box outrage expressed by advocates of Bugs Bunny, Brer Rabbit, Peter Cottontail, the Easter bunny and Rabbit automobiles?

I believe that, given the choice, most of us would take Teddy Roosevelt and his Bull Moose rather than Jimmy Carter and his rabbit!

Wooden Rabbit Hops Around, Sees the U.S.

A rabbit-napper is apparently loose in the Baltimore area. The September 9 *Dayton Daily News* reports that a wooden rabbit used as a lawn ornament had been stolen from its owners last December, but then mysteriously reappeared in August, propped on the windshield of their car. Beside it was a bag of 48 photographs depicting the travels of the bunny.

The perpetrators of this *hare*-brained idea snapped a series of photos of the rabbit. One showed him building a sand castle. Others depicted him at a bus station, an airport, the Wright Brothers Museum in Kitty Hawk and Disney World. He was even photographed with the mayor of Baltimore, Kurt Schmoke.

Three generations of Uncle Wiggly players, limited to moving Uncle Wiggly a few squares at a time on a game board, should be fascinated to know that the subject of this crime hopped to Utah; Kansas City, Missouri; Reno, Nevada; New York; Philadelphia; Atlantic City, New Jersey; Annapolis, Maryland; and St. Thomas.

We must hope that copy cat (make that copy rabbit) crimes do not occur, moving westward from Baltimore through the Miami Valley.

However, all's well that ends well. The owners, Harry and Louise West, appeared on ABC's *Good Morning America* on September 11. They were all smiles as they explained the event. Their rabbit, complete with photos, is now famous and no doubt enhanced in value. It had left Baltimore as a dumb bunny and returned a sophisticated traveler. Maybe there actually is a "victimless" crime.

Historic Dog "Tails" Liven Up White House

After the end of the first year of the Bush White House, it is appropriate to review important events, such as the patter of little feet.

It was a delightful sound and we, at the grass roots, were encouraged. We expected this. We had been told that starting January 20, 1989, we would see a new White House. It would be more casual.

However, the little feet did not belong to the Bush grandchildren, but rather to puppies born to the First Dog, Millie. Not all of the excitement during inauguration week was focused in Washington. For at the same time, Millie was planning a family and getting acquainted with Tug III at his Kentucky farm.

Barbara Bush wrote about the "six-pack" and their home in the White House in the May 1989 issue of *Life* magazine. The First Dog was named after Barbara's good friend Mildred Kerr. "Millie (the dog, not the friend) goes to the Oval Office every morning at 7 and has a little visit there, a little spoiling, and plays a bit and then comes home."

Through the years, the White House has sheltered almost everything that can walk, crawl, swim, slither or fly. These pets have spanned the alphabet from an alligator (John Quincy Adams) to a zebra (Theodore Roosevelt).

To document all of these would be a Herculean task. So at this time, let's just *paws* long enough to look at some of the dogs who have claimed the White House as home.

Material about the following dogs, except for Checkers, was found in a book by Margaret Truman, entitled *White House Pets*. These are not *shaggy dog* stories but actual *tails* of real dogs.

"Pushinka," meaning "fluffy" in Russian, was a gift to Caroline Kennedy from Nikita Krushchev. Pushinka hailed from a notable background. Her mother was Strelka, the first Russian dog to orbit in space. A bit of criticism centered on the fact that the dog was communist. Additionally, opponents of the gift said that Pushinka possibly contained germs that could start a plague or that she might have been implanted with a small transmitter that could send messages back to Russia. However, after successfully passing a physical at Walter Reed Hospital, Pushinka became a favorite at the

Kennedy White House. She and Charley, a White House regular, produced four pups.

Fala was a black scotty puppy given to President Roosevelt in 1940. FDR and Fala became inseparable at the White House, Hyde Park, New York and Warm Springs, Georgia. Fala indisputably logged more travel miles than any other presidential dog. His most important trip came in August 1941. Aboard the U.S.S. Augusta, he sat at the feet of FDR and Winston Churchill while the Atlantic Charter Pact was written.

But Fala was destined to become involved in politics. In 1944, the Republicans started a rumor that Fala had inadvertently been left behind in the Aleutian Islands and that a destroyer went back to pick him up, at a taxpayer expense of $16,000. But the Republicans had forgotten that Roosevelt had a way with words, especially in his famous fireside chats.

Under the circumstances, he understandably might have made a *dogmatic* statement defending himself. In his next radio message, FDR pointed out that the Republicans had not been content with attacks on his wife, his sons and himself, but now were attacking Fala.

"Well, of course, I don't resent attacks, and my family doesn't resent attacks ...but Fala does resent them," he said. He went on to remind his listeners that Fala was Scotch and that "his Scotch soul was furious" about the alleged waste of money. Fala outlived FDR by seven years and now lies in a grave in Hyde Park near his master.

Checkers was never a White House dog, but he did become famous in 1952, when disclosure of a secret "Nixon fund" placed Nixon's second place on the ticket in jeopardy. Nixon took to the airwaves to explain the fund and his personal finances.

After disclosing his income, assets and liabilities, Nixon said, "One other thing I probably should tell you, because if I don't they'll probably be saying this about me too, we did get something—a gift—after the election. A man down in Texas heard Pat on the radio mention the fact that our two youngsters would like to have a dog.

"And, believe it or not, the day before we left on this campaign trip we got a message from Union Station in Baltimore saying they had a package for us. We went down to get it. You know what it was? A little cocker spaniel dog in a crate that he sent all the way from Texas. Black and white spotted. And our little girl, Trisha, the six-year-old, named it Checkers. And you know the kids love the dog and I just want to say this right now, that regardless of what they say about it, we're gonna keep it." (It is interesting to note that no one was trying to take the dog from the Nixons).

A deluge of letters and telegrams was received at the Republican National Headquarters and Ike kept Nixon on the ticket. The speech became know as the "Checkers Speech."

Much more could be said about presidential dogs, but I don't want to *hound* you to death.

My final words are to Millie in the Bush White House. The office of President of the United States is the most burdensome and demanding job known to man. Quite often it is a lonely job. Please keep wagging your tail and making those daily trips to the Oval Office. President Bush deserves whatever small diversion you can give him.

Kids' Four-Legged Gift Got Our Goat

I thought you might like to hear about the visitor that came to our house. It started with our daughters Martha and Nancy shouting, "C'mon, Dad. Come out to the driveway where all the action is."

They sounded insistent.

Stepping onto the driveway, I noticed my daughter Amy gathering up a baby goat in her arms and setting it down in front of her younger sister, Phebe, who was looking on with amazement.

I began to wonder whether I really wanted to add a goat
to our family circle.

My mouth dropped open.

"It's okay, Dad," said my daughter Rebecca. "Amy and I are giving it to Phebe as a gift."

I began to wonder whether I really wanted to add a goat to our family circle, which up until now had consisted of a father, mother, seven children and numerous pets.

"Don't worry about it, Dad," said Amy. "Rebecca and I have been planning this for over a year."

"That may be," I said, "but I didn't get any advance notice. After all, your Mom and I planned on each of you for nine whole months."

I started thinking intently, which is hard to do when a strange goat is licking your hand. I needed desperately to organize my cross-examination.

For starters, I tried this: "What are you going to do if it barks? After all, we have to think of the neighbors."

Amy came to life. "Don't be silly, Dad. Goats don't bark. What they do is bleat. It's a sound sort of between a sheep and a calf."

It was my turn again. "I don't even think you can have a goat in town. There's something in our deed restrictions that says you can't have any horses, cattle, sheep, goats, ducks, chickens, etc. Also, I'm sure the City of Kettering has an ordinance against goat farming."

Next Phebe sprang into action. "Laws like that are unconstitutional. Don't you keep up on this sort of thing? Besides, it's not even as big as our neighbor's dog and it's twice as cute. After all, goats have rights, too."

Next, my wife, Mary, had her say. "The next thing we know, you'll be telling us that it will be a great *watchgoat* and will protect our property from intruders."

In the meantime, the goat was standing on the narrow grassy strip between the driveway and woods. It was nibbling vigorously at some weeds that were two feet tall in the adjoining wooded area.

"See, Dad," Amy said. "It'll keep the woods trimmed for you

and it won't cost you a penny."

"Oh yes it will," I responded. "I'll bet it costs more to buy food for a goat than to buy gasoline for a lawnmower. Furthermore, my riding mower won't leave messes to step on in the woods."

"And I know what else is going to happen," I continued in my very authoritative voice. "A neighbor is going to call the police. Then they're going to come out here and take the goat away. There's always someone trying to get your *goat*."

Rebecca's eyes sparkled. "And there might be a *kid*napper in the neighborhood, too."

"I just remembered," said Rebecca. "The lady we bought the goat from said it would be lonely for the first few days and nights and that we should put a radio near it and play rock music all night."

I was happy to know that some good use had finally been found for rock music.

"Also," chimed in Amy, "the first few nights we each need to get up to check the goat at hourly intervals. We need to see if it's okay—make sure it's not tangled in its chain—comfort it and see if there's enough food. Now, I'll take the midnight shift; Dad, you can take 1 a.m., Mom, you can take the..."

"Oh, no," said Mary. "The last time I got up for a 2:00 a.m. feeding was in 1970 when Phebe was a baby. I'm not going to start that again."

I was trying desperately to think of some pluses. Suddenly, it came to me.

Goat milk!

We'll have lots and lots of goat milk. It's supposed to be good for you. We could even make goat milk fudge and sell it to balance off the cost of food.

But the idea of goat milk was of short duration. Just then, Phebe came by and said, "He's so cute. I'm going to call him Alex.

Alex was the Cecil family's pet during the spring and summer of 1983. In the fall, he was donated to The Learning Tree Project.

VIII

CHRISTMAS COMES BUT ONCE A YEAR!

Christmas Eve Revisited
'Twas the week after Christmas
And all through the house,
The place was a mess
And not fit for a mouse.

Christmas has changed over my lifetime. I remember as a young man, hearing the deep melodious voice of Bing Crosby crooning *White Christmas*. And while this classic is still with us, we now also hear the airwaves filled with songs like *Grandma Got Run Over by A Reindeer*.

The beautiful wonderment of Christmas is still enjoyed by parents and children alike. But Christmas has become a commercial bonanza. Parents still take their kids to the department store Santa and the little tykes still spout off a list—often quite long and memorized—of toys they expect to see under the Christmas tree.

But nervous parents are noting the wishes of the little ones and trying to remember if they have any charge cards that aren't "maxed out." They hope the kids will forget some of the things by Christmas morning. Perhaps the beleaguered parents can stretch the payments out until Easter. Maybe even on Christmas morning they can explain to the little ones, "Santa brought you half of what you wanted. You'll probably get the other half next Christmas."

But we live in a more complex society than we used to. What happens when the little ones discover there really isn't a Santa Claus, Easter Bunny or Tooth Fairy. These days they might go to lawyers to represent them against their parents and to seek damages for the redress of wrongs. Charged with misrepresentation, what could a parent plead at his or her probation hearing? "Judge, I was just having jolly good sport! My parents did that to me and that's why I inflicted it on my kids."

My poem on page 112 pokes fun at Christmas letters. But I want to make this *perfectly clear*—It's not *your* letters I'm jesting about. Actually it's everyone else's letters. If you are presently mailing me Christmas letters, please continue. I like them.

Through all the tinsel and trappings at Christmas, as well as the hustle and bustle, the shopping, with its sound of the cash register, the parties and merriment, we need to remember Bethlehem on that holy night. The "x" in Xmas is not an unknown quantity but rather the Christ child.

Christmas can also change lives. Charles Dickens' Scrooge, after his conversion, said, "I will honor Christmas in my heart, and try to keep it all the year." But Tiny Tim probably said it best: "God bless us every one."

Fruitcake—A Culinary Calamity or Food from the Garden of Eden?

The overwhelming watershed issue dividing us at Christmas time is not whether or not we believe in Santa Claus, or whether to buy a live or artificial Christmas Tree, but whether or not we like fruitcake. Americans have had a love or hate relationship with fruitcake from time immemorial.

This culinary calamity has taken its "hits" for many years. It has been referred to as a bad joke—something to be used as a doorstop or missile. Its detractors have urged the Food and Drug Administration to require warning labels as follows: "Contents are harmful. If swallowed, call your physician immediately. Eating fruitcake can cause serious consequences, such as broken teeth." Any truthful person will tell you that the only way to slice fruitcake is with a chainsaw and that it can only be dented with a backhoe.

I will be honest with you, folks. Up front I will tell you I HATE

I will try to get a law on the books
banning fruitcakes in Ohio

fruitcake. I will not bake, bite into, buy, sell, send, receive, harbor or befriend, in any manner, a fruitcake. After all, if the President and Commander-in-Chief of the whole USA can hate broccoli, I figure I can hate fruitcake. I honestly believe that anyone who likes fruitcake should be probated and have a guardian appointed.

Fruitcake also takes its lumps from humorists. Johnny Carson said he had come to the conclusion that there was only one fruitcake and that people kept giving it to each other. (Come to think of it, when is the last time you saw anyone actually eating fruitcake?) Later Carson confided that someone gave him a brick from the Berlin Wall and that he threw it away, thinking it was just another fruitcake.

Erma Bombeck wrote about this distasteful disaster, in a recent colum, recounting a conversation with her husband, Bill:

Bill: "You are turning into one of those fruitcake people—the ones who are always stuffing a piece of dough with 35 dead fruits baked in it into your mouth and saying, 'But this one is moist.'"

Erma: "How dare you compare me to fruitcake people. They're sick!"

Bill: "You're getting there."

In attacking fruitcake, I decided I should determine its origin. *The Random House Dictionary of the English Language* (Second Edition, unabridged) shows that the word came into common usage around 1840-1850. But an article in *The New York Times*, October 18, 1989, says "Fruitcakes date at least to the Romans, who blended raisins, pine nuts, pomegranate seeds and honey wine into a cake known as 'satura.'" It is my contention that some of the ancient Roman fruitcakes are still in circulation in this country. Indeed, instances of "family fruitcakes" have been uncovered where the cake takes on an antique status and is willed from one generation to the next without ever being actually eaten.

I had to think a long time to come up with any socially acceptable benefits derived from fruitcakes. Here are two: (1) They give columnists something to write about around Christmas and (2) They serve as a measure of incompetence: i.e., someone is a "fruitcake" or he or she is "nuttier than a fruitcake." (It just doesn't sound right to say someone is nuttier than a hot fudge sundae).

My research into fruitcakes uncovered a fact that you as a tax-payer should know. The Defense Department in 1986 sent 75,000 pounds of fruitcake to 2.2 million servicemen and women. The specifications for the holiday treat, according to *Time* magazine, consumed—this is true!—18 pages.

I have decided to take strong executive action against fruit-cakes. I will try to get a law on the books outlawing fruitcakes in Ohio and further prohibiting their interstate shipment.

Thanks for listening as I spout off about fruitcakes. Now get on with something fun like addressing Christmas cards or baking a fruitcake. Whoops! Make that Christmas cookies.

'Twas the Week after Christmas

'Twas the week after Christmas
And all through the house,
The place was a mess
And not fit for a mouse.

The stockings were thrown
On the floor in a heap.
I had a headache,
My wife couldn't sleep.

Now, Mom in her housecoat
And I in my jacket
Were scratching our heads,
Asking how we could hack it?

The bills were piled high,
In a stack on the floor.
I took one grim look
And then split for the door.

We tore up our charge cards.
They lay there in shreds
While visions of bankruptcy
Danced through our heads.

The toys were all broken
And laying around.
The nice talking dolly
Made nary a sound.

And the sled that before
Was shiny and new,
Had now been run over
And broken in two.

The brand new fish tank
Was leaking and crumby.
The nice Christmas guppies,
Now in the cat's tummy.

My Christmas bow tie
Was out of its box.
I found it beneath
My kids' dirty socks.

My wife's Christmas candy
Was stuck to the wall.
My kids were all yelling,
Engaged in a brawl.

The Christmas tree stood in the corner all wilted,
Its ornaments broken, the star on top tilted.

The Christmas tree stood
In the corner all wilted,
Its ornaments broken,
The star on top tilted.

The tinsel was strewn
From basement to attic.
The new CB radio
Brought in only static.

"Christmas is great,"
I said with a leer.
But of course I'm happy
It comes once a year."

As the curtain comes down
In our post Yuletide joint,
I wonder if maybe
We've missed the whole point.

For if you listen
You will probably hear:
"We'll do it all over,
At Christmas next year."

Be On the Lookout for Man in Red Suit

As Christmas approaches, it is only fitting and proper that I should remind you of the dangers to person and property inherent in the season. For example, be alert to:

• Breaking and Entering: Down the chimney St. Nicholas

111

came with a bound.
• Assault and Battery: Jack Frost nipping at your nose.

• Violation of Fire Code: Chestnuts roasting on an open fire.

• Blackmail: He's making a list and checking it twice; gonna find out who's naughty and nice.

• Failure to Properly Fence Wild Animals: Grandma got run over by a reindeer.

Have a safe Christmas!

No Letters, Please

Dear Ebeneezer and Hortense:

Your annual Christmas letter,
I plan to read in stages.
For it is filled with detail,
Containing four typed pages.

So glad to hear that little Chip,
At two can tie shoe laces
And Buffy, quite the young lady,
Has now got rid of braces.

The twins, you write, are in prep school.
They both deserve your praise.
They play first string in soccer,
And always get straight A's.

The skiing trip to Vail, you said,
Was a cure for winter boredom.
Six vacations must be great,
But how can you afford 'em?

And Buffy in state competition
Won first place with her flute.
But I'm yawning as I read,
And don't quite give a hoot.

Hearty congratulations, Bill,
For your seminar at college.
Your audience sat enthralled,
Impressed with your great knowledge.

You may keep us on your letter list,
Tell us of your kids' each sneeze
Let us know who goes to Harvard,
And when they get their PhD.'s.

But before I tackle paragraph two,
I'll lay your letter in my lap.
I am completely underwhelmed.
I think I'll take a little nap

Letter to Santa Claus: No One is Safe From Litigation

Santa Claus
North Pole 122592

Dear Santa:
    With the approach of Christmas and your anticipated trip to
the Miami Valley, I feel I should warn you of problems that have

113

developed since last year. As you know, we are living in a litigious society. Here's where you stand:

KASC (Kids Against Santa Claus) This is a kids' union banded together with two basic complaints:

First, they claim that you have breached contracts you made in various department stores, in that you have failed to deliver certain electric trains, bicycles, dolls, Nintendo sets, etc. that you promised. The kids are tired of waiting.

Second, they charge you with misrepresentation, in that in one night you could not possibly deliver toys to the whole world (not even to just Ohio) and therefore must be a fake. If you enter the homes of KASC members, you do so at your own risk, including a "treat" of stale cookies and rotted carrots for the reindeer.

KASC formed right after last Christmas when one of the kids in a department store tugged at your beard and it came off in her hand.

FAA: The Federal Aviation Authority claims that you have never filed a flight plan showing your estimated time of departure and arrival and a listing of all your stops with the amount of time spent at each. Further, your sleigh is not equipped with even basic safety equipment, such as an altimeter, seat belts and flotation devices.

UAW: The United Auto Workers point out that your sleigh doesn't bear a union label. They further suspect parts of it are made in Japan.

Building Inspection Department: The Chief Inspector claims that each roof on which you land must be reinforced with steel and must be of the same specifications as a helipad. As you know, the situation is further aggravated in that, while you are delivering gifts, the reindeer are "prancing and pawing with each little hoof."

SPCA: The Society for the Prevention of Cruelty to Animals has noted the red nose of your lead reindeer. It is felt that you are exposing him to freezing weather without a proper noseguard.

IRS: Internal Revenue's regulations provide that the snacks you get are actually "income in return for your work." They are demanding that you file a 1040-ES and pay up four times a year.

ICC: The Interstate Commerce Commission has determined that you cross state boundaries with your pack and therefore are subject to its jurisdiction. You have not made proper applications for interstate travel.

County Prosecutor: The Prosecutor has discovered that you are entering some homes without permission, bringing large quantities of soot with you. He is considering a charge of breaking and entering.

ADA: The American Dietetic Association claims that you've had a weight problem for many years. No one should have "a little round belly that shakes when he laughs like a bowl full of jelly." You are a bad example for both the kids and their parents. You should immediately go on a weight reduction diet of 1,800 calories a day.

Rainbow Coalition: This group insists that the elves who make toys throughout the year are not politically correct. They point out that your labor force has no women, no seniors and no people of color.

EPA: The Environmental Protection Agency is preparing a complaint against you. You need to check the emission control system of your reindeer. Numerous complaints have been filed because of reindeer droppings, mainly in residential areas.

You should be aware that pickets from most of the above organizations are at all shopping malls in this vicinity. They are asking for a boycott of all department stores employing Santas.

In spite of the aforementioned obstacles, I hope you will still visit our area. I fervently believe in you and all you stand for. You see, when I was five years old, I found a wonderful electric train in front of my fireplace.

Merry Christmas!
Tom Cecil

IX

LEFTOVERS—
A SMORGASBORD OF THE ORDINARY

Ode to a Self-Service Store
Wouldn't it be nice
To find a clerk amongst the merchandise?

It is a certainty that food remaining from Sunday dinner will inevitably end up in your lunch box Monday morning or else be the anchor for your dinner Monday evening. These second-time-around morsels are commonly called "leftovers." Checking the refrigerator, you might opt to find a dinner meeting rather than confront yesterday's food again.

Leftovers are part of the American way of life, but like stew—what's in it?—you probably should approach leftovers with a degree of caution. The following columns share only one thing—they all are truly leftovers that defy ordinary classification.

But not all leftovers are tasteless. I hope that at least some of these columns will turn out to be a smorgasbord of delights for you.

I'm Going to Stop Procrastinating Starting Next Week

I was going to write this column on procrastination three years ago but waited until now. I noticed that I was sipping lemonade on the patio as I was writing thank-you letters for Christmas presents. After doing this three consecutive years, I felt that I might have a problem with procrastination. It seemed I put things off in other areas of my life as well, usually not adding oil until the light appears on the dashboard for instance. My kids claim I would be a half hour late for my own funeral if I could figure out some way to do it. I looked around for a support group and ran across The Procrastinators Club of America. Club members try to see the humorous side of procrastination and pride themselves in delay.

For example, an article in the *Wall Street Journal* (May 13, 1991) claims that members of the club flew to England to demand a refund from White Chapel Foundry, the maker of the Liberty Bell, because the bell cracked in 1835. "We got a lemon," their signs read. Not to be outdone, the bell maker offered a refund, if they returned the bell in its original packaging.

Other of the group's antics included going to Chicago recently to extinguish the Great Chicago Fire, protesting the War of 1812 during the height of Vietnam and making flawless new year's predictions one year after the fact.

The president of the club, Les Waas, owns an advertising agency in Philadelphia. He claims, "You can't avoid procrastination, so the best you can do is live with it." Waas says his group has 500,000 members but only 9,000 have gotten around to joining. Joining the club costs $16 and annual dues are $5.

Are there any benefits to procrastination? An August 1987 *Readers Digest* article claims there is a positive side to procrastination. For example, while putting off preparation of your tax return until the last minute, you do your spring housecleaning. Thus, many useful small jobs may be completed while waiting to tackle the big one.

Additionally, some problems solve themselves if you delay long enough. I thought of nine examples:

1. The contents of the drawer you didn't throw out 25 years ago now holds baseball cards worth $500.
2. The giant, seven-year-old dust balls behind the couch are now gone because your house burned down.
3. The skirt or bow tie you didn't throw out ten years ago is now back in style.
4. You didn't buy glasses for nearsightedness as a teenager, but now you are farsighted and need buy only one pair

of glasses.

5. You no longer need to answer Uncle Elmer's two-year-old letter since he died last week.

6. You lucked out in not painting the house for ten years, since the state just appropriated your land for highway purposes.

7. The snow you didn't shovel last week melted by itself a few days later.

8. The 50 pounds you never lost resulted in your being hired as a department store Santa Claus.

9. You wisely delayed buying one of the first ball point pens for $10 and now can buy all you want for 49 cents each.

A final note on the Procrastinators Club of America: Sears became irritated when procrastinators insisted on ordering a buggy for $38.90 from an 1898 catalogue.

As for me, I'm trying to decide whether or not to join the club. Maybe I'll send in my dues before the end of the year.

Men: You Auto Trash That Heap

Men and women are different.

Men bond with their cars much like women bond with their newborn babies. The older the car, the stronger the bond. It's in our genes, fellows.

A local friend of mine fell in love with his 1964 Pontiac LeMans. An otherwise intelligent, educated man, his eyes light up when he talks about it.

"You take good care of it, treat it nice, keep it washed up and it will be real good for you." Actually, I'd never claimed his car had body odor.

He takes it out once or twice a week to "exercise" it. Each trip offers an adventure with uncertainty as to whether the car will make it home or be towed away.

Women, on the other hand, consider a car a disposable object. They have no more problem discarding a gas-guzzling, rust-worn heap than they do throwing out the living room couch dented in from too much Monday Night Football and smelling like stale peanuts.

My mother-in-law owned a vintage Chevy. It reached the point where the problems outweighed the benefits. On sudden impulse, she gave it to the Goodwill when they stopped by her home to make a routine pickup of household items.

My own rocky relationship with cars demonstrates a long-standing ignorance of auto mechanics. If car abuse were a crime, I'd be put away for 15 to 25 years with no hope of parole. I've always felt that what's under the hood is none of my business, but rather GM's. I once looked under the hood of my '86 Buick, a two-year-old when I bought it. I found a mishmash of rubber tubes, wires and strange parts, some stacked three deep. Frankly, I wouldn't know a rocker arm from a catalytic converter, and when the words "service engine soon" light up on my dash, I ask the mechanic how much it will cost to turn it off.

My 1975 Olds, a beautiful vehicle, had been driven only by a little old judge, my father, to church and work. Blessed with low mileage, it was given to me upon his death in 1982. For a while it served as the best car in our fleet, driven proudly to church and on family vacations. Gradually, through benign neglect, it deteriorated until finally I hauled building materials in it. But sentiment prevailed. At a time when final rites were in order, and with insurance costing more than the car's value, I got a brainstorm.

"You see, Tommy," I explained to my nephew, "you will be a third generation Cecil to own Grandpa's car. It's yours free!" I turned over a placemat as we ate dinner and listed on it 17 known things wrong with the car. He likes to tinker with cars. I hope he'll give it to his son some day.

My oldest daughter, Amy, recently gave me some daughterly

If car abuse were a crime, I'd be put away for 15 – 25 years
with no hope of parole.

advice about my '86 Buick:

> Amy: "Dad, you should get rid of that bucket of bolts before it disintegrates or bankrupts you."
>
> Me: "Yeah?"
>
> Amy: "Yes, for about $15,000 you could get a dependable little Ford or Chevy with a five-year warranty and you wouldn't have any more worries."
>
> Me: "Impossible!"
>
> Amy: "Why?"
>
> Me: "I paid $15,000 for my first house!" (Admittedly, sticker shock and sentiment prevail in my case.)

In the meantime I think I'll call Tommy and see how Grandpa's '75 Olds is doing.

Monkeying Around with Your Computer

I definitely had an inferiority complex brought on by my computer. My input wouldn't put in; my output wouldn't put out; my boot wouldn't boot up; my cursor wouldn't curse. Obviously, I was depressed.

Ann Landers would have said, "I recommend immediate counseling, dear. Good luck and let me know how it works out."

It's no wonder I was dejected. My computer was far superior to me in many areas.

Take, for example, spelling. After dictating for 40 years, I became reckless, often scurrying to the dictionary for help. However, the "spellcheck" on my computer not only highlights misspelled words, but also offers handy suggestions for instantaneous corrections. With its 115,000-word vocabulary, my PC could win any spelling bee hands down. The *World Book* says that the average adult has a usage vocabulary of 10,000 words and a recognition

My input wouldn't put in; my output wouldn't put out;
my boot wouldn't boot up; my cursor wouldn't curse.

vocabulary (listening and reading) of 30,000 words.

Another area is memory. I have reached the age where I can't always place a name with a face. At these times I go through the alphabet, starting with "A," hoping through association to come up with the right name. My PC, however, flaunts a perfect memory. A two-hour free course coming with the computer barely fazed me. After 30 minutes, the instructor and I parted company, leaving me with a puzzled look on my face and my finger on the exit key. The main thing I learned was the computer is smarter than I and contains many untapped secrets.

Part of the problem involved forcing into my cranial cavity a whole new language known as "computerese." Some of the language consists of acronyms such as DOS (Disk Operating System), RAM (Random Access Memory) and ROM (Read Only Memory). There were other teasers such as "environmental variable path." What is it? What can you do with it? Is it catching? How can you get rid of it? Is it politically correct? The keyboard itself was intimidating with its function, control, delete and alt keys together, with a page up, page down and arrow keys pointing north, south, east and west.

My complex was not helped in the least when one of my kids invaded my house while I was gone and placed a stuffed toy monkey at my computer desk. Beside it was a sign reading, "Dad, if he can do it, you can too!" A few days later a postcard arrived with a monkey's picture on the front. On the reverse side was a message stating, "Dad, it's time to start monkeying around with your computer." This was unusual since the kids were not raised to be offensive. Still I felt as Erma Bombeck must also have felt when she wrote, "Computers aren't for everyone, and there's no doubt in my mind that I will be the last person to acknowledge a terminal as anything more than where you catch an airplane It's nothing I'm proud of, it's just that I don't know how I'm going to survive the computer age." (*Reader's Digest* [Canadian], October, 1987, p. 137 A).

During the first week of January, and as the result of a new year's resolution, I reasoned that the bark of the machine was worse than its *byte*. I received two hours of instruction on each of two consecutive days. This was hands-on, over-the-shoulder training, at the end of which I was "computer literate," if only in the most elementary form. I need many more hours of coaching. My newly acquired ability reminded me of a day years ago when I burst into the house shouting, "Hey, Mom, I can read!"

My advice to other novices is to get guidance from an expert as soon as possible and be patient with yourself. Such patience eluded Don Katz, author, writing in the May 1990 issue of *Teckno Culture*. Under the title "Don't Be Mean To Your Machine," the author asks, "Have computers become too complex to keep their users friendly?" Katz describes a temper tantrum he had over his machine: "In the early fall of 1983, I hauled off and punched a computer. It was two months after I'd purchased my first machine and ten minutes after I'd somehow relegated an entire chapter of a book I was writing to the eternal limbo of the data void. My work was gone forever—vaporized because in my abiding naivete, I'd relinquished control to a machine I didn't understand." Later in the article the author mentions an expert came in and retrieved the "lost" chapter.

I mention the Katz catastrophe to urge patience on your part and to assure you relief is at hand. Built into the Windows program are relaxing games such as solitaire, minesweeper and gorilla. In gorilla, you hit primates on the back with bananas—this is true—and they disappear. When all the gorillas are gone, or your boss comes by, whichever occurs first, the game is over.

If you and your computer are not on friendly terms, "boot up" and get going. If I can do it, you can too!

Pack Rat Takes Initial Steps Toward Dejunking Life

On September 13, 1988, I vowed to lose 44 pounds by the end

of the year. I felt confident of my success. In fact, I made the mistake of sharing my goal with other people, reasoning that this would strengthen my resolve.

You have probably guessed that I not only missed the mark, but missed it by a wide margin. What you wouldn't guess, however, is that the pounds I was trying to lose were not attached to me, but were actually in a plastic bin and consisted of "things that needed sorting, filing and—for the most part—discarding." To lose the pounds would not require a drastic Oprah Winfrey diet, but rather a commitment to confronting an accumulation of many years. As I gritted my teeth and set my goal, the accumulation was actually growing instead of diminishing.

First, I must say that *people* are more important than things. However, having said that, I confess that in my case *things* run a close second. As long as I can remember, I have been a compulsive saver. At the risk of appearing unpatriotic, I admit to sympathizing with Imelda Marcos. Granted, the lady had a tad too many shoes, but it could happen to anyone who buys and accumulates and then forgets to discard.

When my wife said "I do," she was not aware of the dowry that came with me. Early on I was labeled a "pack rat." Curious, I scurried to the dictionary as a mouse scurries after cheese. Here I learned that a pack rat was "any of various small North American rodents that collect in their nests a great variety of small objects." I was even less encouraged when I read the slang definition: "An eccentric collector of miscellaneous objects."

Mine was always the dresser drawer that wouldn't shut, the closet with an open-at-your-own-risk sign, the garage that wouldn't hold a car, the pencil drawer with ten "Keep Cool with Coolidge" pencils stuffed in it and a workshop with enough odds and ends to start a neighborhood hardware store. Although no sticker is pasted on my bumper, my car does "stop for garage sales." I also acquire treasures at auctions. Thus, I may have some of *your* things stashed in boxes, barrels and trunks.

Who else, my wife patiently asks, would save his wisdom teeth in an envelope with the extraction date on it, or a World War II booklet on how to grow a Victory Garden, or an undelivered note to my kindergarten teacher explaining my absence on October 4, 1933, or a snow tire for an extinct car, or a "free" stick from a Brown Giant ice cream bar, or all *Readers Digests* from May 1955 to the present and *Boys' Life* magazines from my four years of scouting.

The real victims of pack ratting, of course, are our loved ones, who see the livable space in the house constantly diminishing. My family has threatened—jokingly, I hope—to dispose of my things when I come to my final resting place. While the earth is opened up anyway, they reason, why not take care of everything at once. However, I am firmly convinced that I can't take my things with me and that my executors must ultimately earn their fee in Probate Court by distributing my personal estate among seven children, the Goodwill and the nearest landfill.

But to "just say no" to accumulating is nigh to impossible for me. I am just guessing that somewhere in the readership of this column there lurks another compulsive saver who needs help. Is there any hope for us? Or as A. Lincoln might query: "Can a house with accumulations from basement to attic still stand?" Let's go through these next few paragraphs together to look for a solution.

First, what to do: The idea is to avoid government intervention. Your home sweet home may be designated "a disaster area" by the federal government. Next, the President, wearing a trench coat, lands in your backyard. The chopper blades are still whirling, blowing his hair out at a rakish angle. As he shakes hands with the local politicians, he glances toward your home and an awesome look of concern steals across his face. The media is here to record this moment in history and you, your house and possessions will make the six o'clock news.

Somewhere there must be a support group to help us. I myself have thought of forming AA (Accumulators Anonymous). Our junk needs to come out of the closet.

Seriously, folks, our best hope lies in a book entitled *Clutter's*

Last Stand. It was written by Don Aslett, who modestly describes himself as "America's No. 1 cleaning expert." Here, in 19 chapters and 276 pages, you can learn about the dreaded disease "junkitis"; you will discover how to "de-junk" your life; you can take the Junkee Entrance Exam to find out whether or not you are a terminal case. You may learn about "committing junkicide," which is strangling yourself with too many possessions. Best of all, if you take Mr. Aslett's advice, you may eliminate your clutter and recapture possession of your home. The book, written in a lighter vein, is profusely illustrated with cartoons.

But I recommend you borrow it from the library instead of buying it. Your bookshelves, like mine, might be overstuffed and sagging.

Let's end on a positive note. Assuming that you don't save old copies of *Times Publications* as I do, you will soon be discarding this newspaper. As you walk toward the trash can, why not pick up one of your sacred things and throw them both away? It will be a wrenching experience, but you will have taken the first step toward dejunking your life.

We both need to lose pounds.

If Wrights Lived Now, They'd Never Get off the Ground

Setting: Kill Devil Hill near Kittyhawk, N.C., on a windy day, December 17, 1903.

Wilbur: "Looks like we got pretty good advice from the Weather Bureau in Washington, D.C."

Orville: "Right, Wilbur. Kill Devil Hill is the best possible location for our flight."

An intruder appears from behind a sand dune.

Intruder: "Good morning, gentlemen. I'm Al Timeter from the Federal Aviation Administration. It

127

has come to our attention that you've been flying gliders here since 1900 and that you're now contemplating an actual power-driven flight."

Wilbur: "Yup."

Intruder: "I want to remind you that federal regulations require that you file a flight plan disclosing your destination, listing your passengers and estimating your time of departure and arrival. Furthermore, looking over your flying machine here, I notice that you are lacking several pieces of basic safety equipment. You don't have an altimeter or even a simple gas gauge. You need ...."

A screeching seagull soars low toward Timeter's head and he departs in a cloud of sand.

Second Intruder: "Hi boys. I'm B. Clean, the park ranger. I don't want to throw cold water on your little project, but I'm here to remind you that this narrow strip of sand has never been zoned for flying, except for birds. Additionally, I see these tools strewn all over, a camera laying there and a tent in the background. I'm going to have to write a citation for littering the beach and camping without a permit."

Wilbur kicks a little sand on Clean's shoes.

Third Intruder: "Are you Wilbur and Orville Wright?"

The boys nod in unison.

Third Intruder: "I'm Reg U. Lation from the Environmental Protection Agency. We're concerned with how you'll dispose of your excess fuel since you haven't filed an environmental impact statement. You can't just dump fuel on the beach, you know. Here's a 10-page application

for a permit and a booklet on how to get rid
of your excess fuel."

Orville rips away the first page of the application, expertly
fashions it into a paper glider and sails it toward Reg.

Fourth Intruder: "Hi, fellows. I'm Chuck Steward, the
union representative for local 123. We have it
on good authority that your engine was made
in a non-union shop in Dayton, Ohio. Our
pickets will be here any time now. We
strongly suggest that you pull that engine and
replace it with one with a union label before
you take off."

Wilbur strums his fingers on the wing and breathes deeply.

Fifth Intruder: "I'm Daniel Dingy, bailiff from Dare
County Probate Court. A group of citizens in
Kittyhawk feel that you two just can't be
playing with a full deck. One of 'em has filed
an application for the appointment of a
guardian for you, based upon mental incom-
petency." (Hands court papers to Wilbur and
Orville.) "Your court date is next Friday at
9:00 a.m. before the Probate Judge."

Orville rotates his index finger around his ear several times
and then points his finger toward Dingy. Wilbur nods his approval.

Sixth Intruder (carrying a bag): "I'm Sue Veneer. I own
Sue's Souvenir Shop just over the second
sand dune (pointing)."

Wilbur and Orville, smiling in unison: "We know—Sue
sells seashells by the seashore!"

Sue: "Right! I've painted a picture of your Wright
Flyer on 50 seashells, which are in this bag. I
hope you'll take them aboard and then au-
thenticate them for me at the end of your
flight. It should help sales immensely."

Wilbur: "I can hardly wait."

Seventh Intruder: "Hi there. I'm Phil Atelic. I'm the duly elected president of the Kittyhawk Philatelic Club. Here are 100 stamped envelopes with a cachet commemorating your anticipated first flight. I was wondering if, as soon as you are airborne, would it be too much trouble if you'd take this rubber stamp and stamp each ..."

Phil drops his envelopes and departs in a scurry of sand as Orville's fingers curl around the handle of a nearby wrench.

Eighth Intruder: "Hi guys. I'm Buddy Upbeat, your friendly disc jockey from station WFLY. Could you fellows say a few words on my tape recorder here? I want to use it on my evening show. I've already thought of a great opening for my many listeners. How's this sound? 'Here are a couple of guys who really have the *Wright* stuff.' (Chuckling) Ha! ha! ha! Do you get it? Do you get it?"

Upbeat's giggles fade and his recorder drops to the ground, as Wilbur goes for a nearby shovel.

Ninth Intruder: "Hi, fellows. I'm Ed U. Cation. I teach first grade over at Kittyhawk Elementary. Next Monday is show-n-tell. You are both invited to our classroom to explain flight to the children. Please bring your flying machine with you. You can park it on the playground."

Orville: "Don't hold your breath!"

Tenth Intruder: "Gentlemen, I'm Matthew Goodperson from the Kittyhawk Chapter of the Moral Majority. Rumor has it that you are about to embark on a great folly—namely, trying to fly through the air with a heavier-than-air

130

machine. Please realize that if the Lord meant
for you to fly, you would have been born with
wings. Why, the very place you have selected
for this misadventure bespeaks the tragedy
you are about to experience. The words "kill"
and "devil" both show that satan is in control
here. Our group passed a resolution..."

Orville rolls his eyes toward the heavens as the two brothers
confer in whispers.

Orville: "Shall we tell him our father's a Bishop in the
               United Brethren Church?"

Wilbur: "No. It would only make matters worse. I've
               got a better idea." (End of whispering.) "Mr.
               Goodperson, here's a summons from the
               Probate Court of Dare County (handing him
               Dingy's papers) requesting that you and all of
               your group appear before the Probate Judge
               next Friday. He'll expect you at 9:00 a.m."

Five minutes elapse.

Orville: "If no more intruders come by, we need to get
               down to the serious business of flying this
               machine."

Wilbur: "Wright! That's 'right' with a "w" Get it, Orv?
               Get it?"

Orville: (Groan.)

Wilbur: "For a while there I thought that with all these
               intruders we should just go back to Dayton
               and build bicycles. It would be a lot simpler
               than this!"

Orville: "Let's stick with it. If we can bring it off,
               maybe they'll name a high school, a univer-
               sity or an Air Force Base after us someday."

Wilbur: "It's only eight days 'til we'll be home for
               Christmas. Let's hope we get our Christmas
               present early—today."

As the scene fades on our determined twosome, a coin is tossed into the Kill Devil sky to determine which brother will make the first flight.

Case of the Musical Molars

The case of the musical molars was reported recently involving a Florida housewife who found that she was receiving music through the bridgework in her teeth. The selection included *It's a Long Way to Tipperary*, *Battle Hymn of the Republic*, *Rambling Rose*, *My Country 'Tis of Thee* and *Pack Up Your Troubles in Your Old Kit Bag*.

In view of the caliber of radio music these days, anyone who can tune in this kind of music merely by opening her mouth should snap up the deal in a hurry!

Practice Crimes—An Idea Whose Time Has *Not* Come

The Sunday *Dayton Daily News* reported strange doings in Charleston, West Virginia— a fake bank robbery to test bank security. Little wonder that the victimized teller filed suit against the bank, the city and the police chief.

It was indeed fortunate that the teller literally was not scared to death. It also was fortunate that the proverbial little old lady customer you always see at the savings bond window did not view the "bandits" through her granny glasses and, sensing her moment in history, draw a gun from her knitting bag and plug the police chief in true Dick Tracy style.

One cannot help but wonder why such a scheme for testing

bank security was devised. If the participants really need this type of therapy, a summer camp could be devised for bankers and police where bank robberies and effective counter measures are planned and carried out.

To add a touch of realism, organized crime might be induced to send real live criminals to take part in the event upon being promised that the participants would be immune from arrest for past crimes while dispensing this public service. There would, of course, have to be an understanding that the bank would use fake money and the criminals fake bullets.

In the meantime, suffice it to say that the Charleston plan for testing bank security probably will not catch on beyond its own city limits.

Reverse Garage Sale—An Antidote for Pack Ratting

I walked from room to room in my house, trying to survey the magnitude of my problem—pack ratting. "Pack rat" is literally defined by Webster as "a rodent of the Western U.S., about six inches long, with a bushy tail. It has plump cheek pouches in which it carries food and things to be hoarded."

My desks were mounded high with stacks of papers, curled at the corners and yellowed with age. The bottom dresser drawer sagged with collections of "things"; in the closet, clothes were packed so tightly that it was almost impossible to pry hangers in or out. The basement, attic and garage also attested to abuse—years and years of accumulation. I was fighting a losing battle. A quick inventory revealed that I was squirreling things away faster than I was discarding them.

I thought, but only momentarily, of throwing things out. Instantly I abandoned the idea since it violated the primary tenet of successful pack ratting: *Never throw anything out.*

Checking with my seven children disclosed that none of them

was a pack rat. Furthermore, they threatened that if they were settling up my "affairs" some day, they would make short shrift of my treasures, trashing most of them and then finding a new home for the balance at the Goodwill. No one desired to pick up my banner of pack ratting and go forward with it.

Admittedly, my house runneth over. My collection was diverse. Take for example the 30-year-old Monopoly game. The kids had thrown out the dice and bought properties by placing the board on the wall and throwing darts. Half the cards and all the money were missing.

The GE toaster, resulting from opening a new savings account back in the Neanderthal period, popped up only black toast. All three shovels were in good shape. The last two, purchased at a garage sale, cost only $1 each. The sign "Beware Of Dog" reminded me of a gentle pet named Lucky, who first lost all his teeth and then checked out. I hadn't owned a dog for 30 years.

Suddenly, a light flashed on. I would have a "reverse garage sale." I would search out a garage sale already in progress in my area and unload my things there. This proved to be confusing to the first garage sale lady (G.S.L.) I encountered:

> Me: I'd like to leave all the stuff in my back seat, in the trunk and on the roof.
>
> G.S.L.: I don't think I can afford it.
>
> Me: No. It's free.
>
> G.S.L.: Impossible! I'll give you $10 for everything.
>
> Me: No. No. No. Take it quickly, please, before I start buying your things.

I have named the above transaction a "reverse garage sale." Neither the name nor the procedure are copyrighted or patented. If you're a pack rat, give it a shot. It may be your last best compromise between sanity and insanity.

Good luck as you confront your precious things.

X

HIT AND RUN POEMS
OR
FROM BAD TO VERSE

Through the years I sent a weekly letter to my children scattered in various cities and states across the country. I wrote a short poem at the end of each letter. Then I accumulated these poems under the title of *Hit and Run Poems or From Bad to Verse*. The idea was that reciting a poem was a "hit," followed by my breaking into a "run" before tomatoes and eggs were launched in my general direction. In other words, I realize that some of these are real *groaners*. In spite of this, I have started each of the preceding nine chapters with a Hit and Run poem.

Note: Hit and Run is a serious offense in Ohio (R.C. 4549.02), punishable by a fine of not more than $1,000 and imprisonment not to exceed six months, or both.

Thus I hope there is a substantial distance between you and me as you read this section.

If pressed in court, I'll plead *nolo contendere*.

Reptilian Ruse
The zoo keeper made a bad mistake
With his unruly rattlesnake.
Picking up an *empty* skin,
He found the snake still lived therein.

Bifocally Speaking
"The print is far too small," she said.
Her needle's getting hard to thread.
Her brow is knit in concentration;
Alas! Bifocal generation.

135

Medical Economics
The med school graduate, Dr. Flick,
Opened his office to heal the sick.
His patients, he found, were not too ill
Until, of course, they got his bill.

KID(ney) Problems
My kids avoid the bathroom
With bladders strong as steel,
Except when vacation starts,
And I'm behind the wheel.

The Law's Delay
The lawyer quoted from his brief,
"My client's certainly not a thief.
And if you find that he did steal,
I'll quickly file a long appeal."

The Centipede
How would you like a hundred feet?
The centipede thinks it's really neat.
The only problem, he confides,
Is when he tries to go down slides
Or rush across a busy street.

Computer Mania
Remember when humans manned all accounts,
And tellers your balance could announce?
But now we hear with studied frown,
"I'm sorry, but our computer's down."

Mower Power to You (Me)
From the comfort of my hammock
For my lawn I plan what's best.
Should I mow from north to south,
Or instead, from east to west?

Hair Today—Gone Tomorrow
To my barber I confide
When I walk into his shop,
"Take a little off the side
And put it on the top."

New Year's Resolutions
One thing on which I hadn't reckoned,
Was how to make it to January second.

Ode to a Pay Phone
Did the guy who took the phone book
And chained it 'neath the shelf,
Ever go into that nook
To use the book himself?

Poet's Lament
(with apologies to Ogden)
You don't like my humor?
My verse is all trash?
At these paltry prices
You can't expect Nash.

Put to Sleep "Ether" Way
The preacher decided that he
An anesthesiologist should be;
Into a new career he leapt
Finally getting paid while people slept.

Catalog Deception
He sent the bathtub back to Sears;
He knew that they had lied.
Because when he uncrated it
The girl was not inside.

Snow Daze
He kneeled beside his bed
And bowed his head to pray,
"Please, Dear Lord, make sure
That there's no school today."

Talked to Death
Oh, members, let us
Have great pity
For the good idea
Sent "to committee."

The Taxidermist
The taxidermist, up for life,
Instead of animals,
Had stuffed his wife.

Toothache
Killing
Drilling
Filling
Billing

Blow Out Blues
How's come the blow out
On one of your new tires
Never happens 'til
The warranty expires?

Suffering Parents

We're used to wrong numbers
And callers obscene,
To rude operators
And salesmen unseen.
But our greatest problem
And worst abuser
Lives right in our house;
She's our teenage user.

Swinging at 50

My double faults are frequent
My lobs don't land, but soar;
The ball comes back much faster,
I can't remember the score.
The net's a little higher now,
My serve's not quite so nifty;
There's lots more court to cover,
Because I'm over 50.

Why *My* Tie?

I have often wondered why
When I wear a brand new tie,
A spot of soup at once appears,
And not on one I've owned five years.

Clipped (Barber Shop Economics)

The balding man sat in the chair,
And thought it wasn't very fair.
He was upset, to be precise,
That he still had to pay full price.

Footballholic
During every football season
He loses all his sense of reason.
He hibernates upon the couch.
She's married to a football grouch.

Freedom From Speech
Speakers who prattle on and on
Should know my concentration's gone.
Though staying awake is my goal,
I just lose all my snooze control.

Frightened? What Fur?
She felt so violated
That he would enter the house.
But I had little sympathy,
For it was just a mouse.

The Traffic Light
Sorry, officer, but don't you see?
That light sure looked green to me.
Well, maybe it was sort of yellow,
But can't you be a human fellow?
My wrong, if any, is quite minimal.
Why not look for some real criminal?

Angler's Dilemma
Fishermen are puzzled
And ask for goodness sake,
Why the fishing's always better
On the far side of the lake.

The Baker

The banker came by the bakery shop
To see if credit he should stop.
When questioned about his poor cash flow,
Replied the baker, "I'm rolling in dough."

Gas for Less

My antique car is great,
In fact it has real class.
And so I wish that I
Could buy some antique gas.

Caught Shorthanded

After taking a letter
She wondered merely,
What came after "Dear Sir"
And before "Sincerely"?

Disrepair

Whenever I run for my tools
My wife always tries to nix it,
Because she knows in the end
The plumber will just have to fix it.

Parts Department

Doctors in the days of yore
Didn't have so many smarts;
'Cause when grandpa's heart wore out,
They didn't have spare parts.

Popcorn

Just when all the rumbling stops
Another kernel up and pops.

The Used Car
The used car salesman was all smiles:
"Here's a beauty with very few miles."
"'Twas owned," he said, "by a little old lady,
Who bought it new in Eighteen eighty."

Let Bag Gones Be Bag Gones
The Eskimo's flight was great;
He happily de-planed in Nome;
But by some strange quirk of fate,
His bags de-planed in Rome.

The Old Codger
At a pace quite slow
His energy spent
His get up and go
Had got up and went.

Weathering the Storm
The weather report I've rated
As far too complicated.
So for me just let me know
Will there be sunshine, rain or snow?

You Light Up My Life
Edison was a genius
To invent the electric light
But we would still be in the dark.
If Franklin hadn't flown his kite.

XI

IN MEMORIAM

Erma Bombeck (1927 – 1996)
Lester L. Cecil (1893 – 1982)

Remembering Erma Bombeck

Her writing style will be remembered along with the country's greatest humorists.

The Bombeck era ended Monday with the untimely death of Erma Bombeck on April 22, 1996. Who was Erma Bombeck?

She tickled the funny bones of millions of Americans with her home-style humor; at first she wrote three, then two columns per week, syndicated in more than 500 papers; she wrote 12 books, most of which made the best-seller list; she wrote a monthly column for *Good Housekeeping;* she was a guest on TV shows; she was in demand as a speaker; she practiced and wrote about family values long before politicians took up the crusade; she spoke for millions of women and made them feel worthwhile in their work at home or away from home; she was a giant among writers, easily earning a place in her lifetime with such "greats" as Mark Twain and Will Rogers. Her humor was universal, transcending age and gender. But most of all, she laughed a lot and made us laugh too.

Erma loved young people and was a popular graduation speaker. In 1988, my daughter, Nancy, and I attended commencement ceremonies at Wittenberg University. Erma was true to form, spicing good solid advice with a sprinkling of humor.

"I gave a speech at Harvard University last spring," she said, "and I said to a group of rather high achievers in law school, 'I hate to depress you but I have seen your future and I'm it. Many of you are destined for successful careers and some of you may even

143

stop off for a short visit to fame. But most of you will live ordinary lives . . . just like the ones I write about. You'll get married and buy a car that won't outlast the payments. You'll spend $2,000 to straighten the teeth of a kid who never smiles anyway. You'll take the family camping where you'll park next to a public toilet and do your laundry in a saucepan and tell everyone you had a wonderful time. And these will be the happiest days in your lives . . . as they were for the parents watching you today.'"

At the conclusion of the service, Erma stayed on until she shook the last hand, autographed the last program, and stood next to the last beaming graduate while the parents snapped a picture. Erma was a very caring person who always gave 100 percent.

She was also blessed with a tremendous capacity for work. She continued to write after serious major surgery three years ago and then more recently while on home dialysis four times a day for a disease known as polycystic kidney disease. Under these adverse conditions she stayed on schedule with her columns, even working ahead, and was writing her thirteenth book before going to the hospital for a kidney transplant.

In 1988 and 1992, in published columns in this newspaper, I suggested, in fun, that Erma throw her "bonnet" into the Presidential primaries. I reasoned that a President Bombeck would create a cabinet position known as Secretary of the Department of Humor and that government in a lighter vein might arouse citizens' interest in the process.

In spite of my sending her campaign buttons such as "Buckeyes for Bombeck" and "Bill For First Man," Erma stuck with what she did best. But she enjoyed the idea and responded in two columns.

In 1988 she wrote, "It started off as a great week. I had my teeth cleaned and there were no cavities. I found my favorite lipstick in an old handbag that I thought was lost. And the daffodil bulbs I planted upside down were pushing through the soil. Then I got a letter from an attorney in Ohio saying he was running me for President of the United States and he is beating the crabgrass roots on my behalf to 'put a little life in the White House....'"

Four years later, in 1992, she wrote, " ... I don't know, Tom, if the party really wants me, I'll think about it and get back to their people. I won't seek the office, you understand, but I won't say absolutely for sure that I'll say yes or no....The bottom line is, I am running. Please send me another shipment of campaign buttons."

Bombeck fans are somewhat addicted and maybe even a little fanatical. Loving Erma is somewhat like admiring motherhood, the American flag and apple pie. So we let our hero go with great reluctance.

But her legacy of humor will live on and be enjoyed by readers not yet born. Her style of writing will be taught in journalism and writing classes in colleges across the country. And we, her fans, will read and reread her books and columns, and they'll delight us as much as when they were first published.

This, indeed, is the end of an era. We'll miss you, Erma.

Time Has Stilled His Hands

The telephone rang at 7:15 the morning after Thanksgiving. It shouldn't have rung, since there was no school for the children. And thus, the call had to be important or unpleasant. I picked up the phone on the bedside stand.

"Mr. Cecil, this is Good Samaritan Hospital. Your father had a restless night. He wants to see his wife and we don't want to alarm her. Would you get the message to her?" A half hour later, I picked up Lucille at her apartment and we headed toward the hospital. I tried to comfort her.

"You know how men are, Lucille," I said. "He just wants you to baby him a little."

Neither of us took much courage from this attempt at levity. I looked at Lucille and could see she was tired from five straight

days of hospital visiting, but was still able to smile. I was happy for the ten beautiful years that Dad and Lucille had spent together.

The sight in room 2040 of the coronary care unit was not reassuring, nor were the consultations with the doctors. Dad was breathing rapidly, with large heaves. He was restless and his voice had a guttural quality. He indeed had spent a restless night.

My brother, Dave, arrived. The three of us kept a bedside vigil. An oxygen mask was placed around his head and over his nose. And then it started—a motion that continued for several hours: Dad's hand trying to pull the oxygen mask away from his face.

I looked at the hands and remembered Christmas in 1932 when they slid together several pieces of track and then screwed them to a board, showing me how to make the shining new Lionel train move around the track.

Again his hand moved to the mask. I smoothed it down to his side and made some stupid comment about having to follow the doctor's orders.

"I want this mask off—just for ten minutes," he said.

I had to cock my head toward his to interpret the garbled message.

I looked at the hands again. When I was a child, they often placed a shiny penny on the window sill by my bed and held me the next morning as I thanked him, feeling that I was the richest kid on the block.

Those hands had taught me how to cast a fishing plug and undo the ever present backlash. They had taught me how to cut down dead elm trees and saw them into firewood.

The hands continued to move toward the mask. Lucille, David and I took turns restraining them. We called it "hand duty." As we held down one hand, the other would start toward the mask, trying to remove it.

"Don't worry, Dad," I said. "We're all right here with you."

"That's the trouble," he said. His sense of humor came through even in this crisis.

I studied his right hand some more. It had shaken the hand of

President Eisenhower in 1953 when Dad was named U.S. District Court judge. It had gaveled crowded courtrooms to silence, turned thousands of pages of law books and carried his briefcase home from work.

Just in October, he had proudly met his colleagues on the U.S. Sixth Circuit Court of Appeals in Cincinnati. I wondered if I would still be working at age 89—24 years past the average retirement age.

The hands again tried to reach the mask. It was heartbreaking to have to overpower them.

"I'm going to go home," he said as he slid his feet toward the side of the bed.

The nurse administered a shot to relax him. It must have worked because he soon said, "We've got to get these things over the fence."

I looked out over Benson Avenue on a rainy, cold November day.

"Over the fence?" I hoped that his mind had spun backward to the early 1900s and that he was on his grandfather's farm on a hot June day doing chores.

Toward the end of the day, the inevitable happened. We were asked to leave the room. Soon the red light was flashing by his door and people in white jackets were scurrying into his room from all directions.

Later we were told that we could go back into the room. The troublesome mask was gone. Dad's hands lay peacefully beside him.

You may order additional copies of

I WANT MY TURN IN THE SHOWER!

by writing to:

> Tom Cecil
> P. O. Box 842
> Dayton, OH 45409

Please send your check or money order for $12.95 per book.

Amount enclosed $_____ for _____ books.

Name _____

Address _____

_____

(Optional) Autograph to:_____

_____